ICT – Integrating Computers in Teaching

GW00600625

David Barr

ICT – Integrating Computers in Teaching

Creating a Computer-Based Language-Learning Environment

PETER LANG

Oxford · Bern · Berlin · Bruxelles · Frankfurt am Main · New York · Wien

Bibliographic information published by Die Deutsche Bibliothek
Die Deutsche Bibliothek lists this publication in the Deutsche Nationalbibliografie;
detailed bibliographic data is available on the Internet at ‹http://dnb.ddb.de›.

British Library and Library of Congress Cataloguing-in-Publication Data:
A catalogue record for this book is available from The British Library, Great
Britain, and from The Library of Congress, USA

Cover design: Thomas Jaberg, Peter Lang AG

ISBN 3-03910-191-9
US-ISBN 0-8204-7176-3

© Peter Lang AG, European Academic Publishers, Bern 2004
Hochfeldstrasse 32, Postfach 746, CH-3000 Bern 9, Switzerland
info@peterlang.com, www.peterlang.com, www.peterlang.net

Printed in Germany

Dedicated to the memory of Miss Pauline Johnston, M.A. (1951–2001), formerly of Cambridge House Boys' Grammar School, Ballymena, Northern Ireland.

Contents

Acknowledgements

I should like to thank Professor John Gillespie, for his constant support, guidance, dedication and professionalism throughout my research. In addition, I express deep gratitude to Professor Angela Chambers and Dr Jane McKee for their support in pursuing the publication of this work. I am also indebted to the staff (both administrative and academic) and students of the Faculty of Modern and Medieval Languages at the University of Cambridge and their counterparts in the Departments of French, Italian and Spanish at the University of Toronto. I wish to acknowledge, in particular, Gavin Burnage and Prof. Russon Wooldridge for their excellent hospitality and support during my research visits to Cambridge and Toronto. Finally, I would like to thank the staff and students in the School of Languages and Literature at the University of Ulster for all their support and their participation in my research study, especially the School Secretary, Mrs Rosemary Moore. Finally, I am grateful to the support and editorial assistance given to me by my good friend, David Anderson.

Introduction

Computer-based learning is a long established area of educational research. In recent years, however, its importance appears to have grown. In the UK, additional impetus has come from Government, particularly through the publication of the Dearing Report into Higher Education in 1997. That report advocated improved provision of ICT facilities for students in third level education because of its belief 'that the innovative exploitation of Communications and Information Technology (C&IT) holds out much promise for improving the quality, flexibility and effectiveness of higher education'.[1]

Consequently, the current educational climate appears to favour the continued integration of computer technology into learning and, therefore warrants a systematic study, through this book. Although this integration is taking place throughout the educational system, from primary to tertiary level, it is the latter where most interest seems to focus and, as a result, this study intends to concentrate on that area. A number of factors support this choice.

At the moment, one of the main trends in higher education is the development of flexible learning. In an educational climate where many undergraduates have to balance academic study alongside undertaking remunerative employment, and distance learning courses enjoy considerable popularity, it appears that universities are responding to a general demand for courses that use flexible modes of study and course delivery, especially through the use of computer technology.

Quality assessment pressures, such as the QAA (Quality Assurance Assessment) in the UK, have led many institutions to develop ambitious plans to use computer technology in learning and teaching,

---

1 Chapter 13, *Dearing Report into Higher Education*, accessed on the World Wide Web, June 2002: http://www.leeds.ac.uk/educol/ncihe/nr_202.htm

as well as increasing ICT provision, in an effort to ensure the best possible score in such assessment exercises.

It can be argued that there is more finance available for the integration of computer technology in education in universities than in schools and, consequently, the development potential is greatest in the tertiary system.

Much has been written in the area of computer-based learning and computer-based learning environments, and it would be impossible to consider this vast area within the limited time frame required for this book. It is, therefore, necessary to focus on specific areas of computer-based learning. The use of computer technology in language learning seems an ideal example. This field is well researched, with vast amounts of articles studying specific computer applications (such as CALL, the Web and computer-mediated communication) and their pedagogical value for language learners. Some researchers consider certain computer applications, such as the Web, as a complete learning environment (Harris 1999: 139–164). In other words, they believe that these applications are all that is required for students to learn successfully. In recent years, considerable research has been conducted in the use of Virtual Learning Environments (VLEs), such as *FirstClass* and *WebCT*. These VLEs offer extensive facilities to learner and teacher, and have proved to be particularly successful in distance education. Some would suggest that these, too, constitute entire learning environments. Nevertheless, they, like all computer applications, have pedagogical limitations and few researchers have investigated how to integrate all these applications together to achieve maximal benefit for the learning process. Richmond (1999: 312) suggested this as an area of future research in computer-based language learning.

Furthermore, much of the current research advocates the use of computer technology in a learning environment because of the pedagogical value of computer applications.[2] It does not seem to consider the role of the human teacher and traditional teaching methods in such an environment. This work therefore intends to bridge some of the gaps in research into computer-based learning, especially language

2   An example of this can be found in K Cameron, (ed.) (1999). *CALL: Media, Design and Applications*, Lisse: Swets & Zeitlinger

learning, that have been described above, by considering whether it is possible to create a learning environment that is based around computer technology, but which may embrace other factors and learning and teaching styles.

In particular, this book will consider the following questions:

1. What is a 'computer-based language learning environment'? What exactly is the role of the computer in this type of environment?
2. What is involved in creating a computer-based environment?
3. Are such environments necessary? Do they work? Do they meet all the needs and expectations of the learners and teachers who use them?

In order to address the above questions, this work has been divided into three parts.

Chapters 1 and 2 consist of a background report on the learning process and study of computer-based learning, with particular reference to language learning, with a view to explaining the concept of a computer-based language-learning environment. This will also help to establish a list of generic factors to be considered in the composition of this type of environment

Chapters 3, 4 and 5 will discuss case study reports on the use of computer-based learning in the languages departments of three separate universities, which may be considered substantially diverse enough in nature and ethos to represent a worldwide sample. This section will illustrate examples of good and bad practice in the creation and implementation of a computer-based language-learning environment.

Chapter 6 analyses the effectiveness of each learning environment, especially with regard to how well these environments meet the needs of language learners and teachers in each institution studied. It offers a basic framework of recommendations for institutions interested in designing a computer-based environment.

Chapter One
What is a learning environment?

Before looking at the role of the computer, let us firstly define what is a learning environment. Educationalists like Diana Laurillard (1993: 280) equate the term with that of 'learning context', which could be interpreted as the circumstances in which the act of learning takes place. It therefore seems appropriate to examine the learning process briefly.

The act of learning

Hilgard and Bower define learning as 'the process by which an activity originates or is changed through reacting to an encountered situation' (1966: 2). An expanded definition is provided by the PacifiCorp Foundation for Learning, who define learning in the following way:

> Learning refers to concerted activity that increases the capacity and willingness of individuals, groups, organizations and communities to acquire and productively apply new knowledge and skills, to grow and mature and to adapt successfully to changes and challenges.[1]

According to this definition, there appear to be two basic steps in the learning process: firstly, the learner acquires information and skills. This is similar to the inputting of data into a computer. On its own, completing this step does not mean that one is actually learning. A second stage in the process is required. The information and skills then need to be processed or applied by the learner. Examples of this

[1] For complete definition, see the PacifiCorp Foundation homepage, accessed January 2003: http://www.pacificorpfoundation.org/Article/Article16920.html

stage include answering a question or using information or skills acquired to solve a problem. Students learn in different ways, although at present there are two principal approaches to learning: the behaviourist and the constructivist.

The behaviourist approach

One of the main characteristics of the behaviourist approach is that learner behaviour is directly influenced by that of teachers (Fontana 1984: 108). In other words, the way in which students learn will depend on what their teachers do and say, as well as opinions and views they might express. Behaviourism advocates the need for teachers to structure the student learning environment to maximise learning potential. In other words, it believes that teachers, as opposed to the learners, have the responsibility for affording learning opportunities, through the provision of stimulus material, such as books, lectures or other sources of reference (Blackman 1984: 9). This means that teachers will have a direct influence over the learning process of their students since they will direct and modify the learning environment. Furthermore, if, for example, they change stimulus material, such as books, this can change the way that students think about certain topics or issues. This suggests that the teacher has control over student learning behaviour.

Teacher control can be considered as both positive and negative in the learning process. Students will not always be highly motivated learners and, as a result, need encouragement and guidance to learn effectively. Behaviourism allows for precision teaching. This enables the teacher to recognise learning difficulties, assess student performance and take necessary action. Raybould (1984: 47) suggests that this is a crucial aspect of the learning process because, since each learner is unique, it follows that each learning experience is also unique. This suggests that all students have particular learning strengths and weaknesses and that there is no one universally effective teaching method. Behaviourism allows the teacher to change methods, perhaps using different stimulus material, such as remedial resources, for example, when learning weaknesses arise. If the teacher did not have the same control over the learning process, he or she would be unable to adapt to students' particular learning needs with the same rapidity.

The ability to control student learning may seem particularly relevant to learning at primary and secondary level. At university, the mature learner takes more responsibility for his learning, which suggests that behaviourism has less of a role in the learning process in that context. Nevertheless, students at that level also need guidance, especially when taking subjects that are completely new to them and which they will study in greater depth than they would at school. In fact, lectures are a good example of behaviourism in action. Students are often required to copy down the points made by the tutor in such a class and these are used to complete essays and other pieces of coursework. Often, the stimulus material used in lectures and similar classes will convey particular viewpoints, which suggests that the teacher is attempting to influence what the students think about certain issues. This can be considered advantageous because many students need a springboard to encourage them to think critically. The directed approach of behaviourism allows the creation of such learning catalysts.

Behaviourism, though, also has some disadvantages. By relying on teacher control of the learning process, less seems to be expected of the students and it is quite conceivable that this will reduce their motivation to learn. Blackman (1984: 7) confirms that students are not considered as active agents in this approach to learning. This implies that the student has a passive role in his learning. One of the dangers of this is that students can become detached from the process and feel demotivated, which, in turn, affects their desire to learn. Some students will prefer to be more active in the way they learn and perhaps work better on their own than under the direction of teachers. Therefore, far from benefiting from the behaviourist approach, these individuals may feel that it suppresses their learning potential.

In addition, a behaviourist approach to learning can also encourage student laziness. This can be seen especially at university level, where frequently students have been known to produce virtually verbatim transcripts of lecture notes in essays or other work, instead of engaging in their own research. This reveals another problem with behaviourism. Students become so reliant on the teacher and the views or opinions he expresses, that they are unable to analyse critically or form opinions themselves. Professor Diana Laurillard believes that undergraduate education is rooted in behaviourist learning. She argues that although undergraduates are encouraged to develop their own viewpoints within a subject and analyse the material they are presented with, when it comes to assessment, such as examinations, tutors will still expect predefined answers (Laurillard 1993: 2). This reveals a further drawback with behaviourism: teachers too may become lazy or at least complacent in their approach to student learning. By expecting predetermined answers, some staff therefore may seem unwilling to encourage students to develop or argue their own viewpoint. If students use traditional and well-known ideas and views in their work, this makes it easier and quicker for staff to mark such work.

The constructivist approach

Until the early part of the last century, behaviourism was regarded as the main approach to learning. As early as the first quarter of the twentieth century, a number of education plans were designed, notably those of Dalton and Winnetka, that questioned the traditional teacher-centred approach. The Winnetka plan, for example, believed in replacing traditional lectures with self-instructive tasks (Lindgren 1967: 390). Given that it is generally considered that the process of acquiring knowledge is 'individually constructed' (Hannafin and Land 1997: 173), many educationalists feel that the student needs to be able to adopt whichever method of acquiring knowledge he finds most effective and comfortable. Constructivist learning is based on this principle: each person has unique potentialities, desires and feelings (Woodruff 1961: 16) and he should process information himself and gain an understanding of it, rather than having ideas thrust upon him by a teacher. In other words, in the constructivist learning approach, the learner is responsible for gaining knowledge and understanding and, consequently, constructs his own process of learning, rather than playing a passive role (Reagan 1999: 415). It is believed that if the learner plays an active role in both acquiring knowledge and pro-

18

cessing it, he will feel an attachment with what he is learning rather than feeling very distant and separated from it: a feeling that can often occur when the learner plays a more passive role in the learning process – a common trait of behaviourist learning.

Timothy Reagan, professor of Educational Studies at the University of Connecticut, in his paper on this learning methodology, defines two forms of constructivism: radical and social (1999: 415). The former is founded on the belief that the learner alone can construct his knowledge and that 'knowledge is not something that is passively received by the learner'; whilst the latter accepts the role of the individual in constructing his own knowledge, it admits that this process should take place within a socio-cultural context. Radical constructivism seems to redefine fundamentally the principle of teaching and learning, to the extent that the teacher does not appear to have a role in the learning process. The latter form though seems to accept the role of other factors, e.g. the physical environment, fellow learners and the teachers in the process of knowledge acquisition and evaluation. Both definitions demonstrate that there are differing approaches to learning. Inevitably, some learners will prefer to work on their own, having the self-discipline and motivation to learn in that context, possibly even viewing the presence of others as an unwelcome distraction. Others will be more socially orientated and will welcome the valuable contribution and perspective that their colleagues bring to the learning process: these learners may lack the self-discipline and motivation to work on their own. In their study on improving student learning, Brian Webb, Clive Cochrane and D R Newman believe that learning is a social phenomenon (1994: 330). They base their assumption on evidence from Rogoff (1990) that a child develops psychologically through interaction with people, hearing new words or expressions, for example. Whether it is a solitary or a social approach to learning, both represent learning contexts where the learner and not the teacher is responsible for his own learning.

Constructivist learning engages the student in the learning process and is normally centred on the learner, as opposed to the teacher. It is also known as 'active learning', and has two primary characteristics: it places the responsibility for learning at the feet of the learner and gives the teacher a different role in the learning process.

With active learning, the learner focuses on his individual cognitive strengths and weaknesses, which encourages him instead of the teacher to find the most suitable and effective learning method (Hannafin and Land 1997: 174). Furthermore, active learning places the responsibility for learning quite firmly with the student, which requires considerable learner maturity (Blin 1995: 57). With active learning, the learner may be presented with some information, from a lecture, for example. It is, however, the responsibility of the learner to study and research the information as appropriate in order to gain a more complete understanding of the information and to interpret it accurately. This constructivist approach is like a chain: learning material represents the links on the chain but it is the responsibility of the learner to join the links of the chain; if one link is weak, i.e. he does not understand a certain concept, he must do what is necessary to make it strong and hence make the whole chain effective. The responsibility of strengthening the student in his weak areas of learning shifts from the teacher who, although pedagogically experienced, is not in the enviable position of knowing intimately the weaknesses of every student he teaches and is generally required, because of time and resources, to focus on the needs of the entire class of learners. According to Davies and Williamson (1998: 10), this shift of learning responsibility from teacher to learner also helps to motivate learners since they become active agents in the learning process, instead of passive recipients of information.

It would be wrong to say that active learning excludes the teacher from the learning process, for he too has a role to play. In university education, where many courses encourage active learning, students still have a substantial level of contact with tutors. In the case of undergraduate courses, the reason for this is clearly understandable: most undergraduate students are aged between seventeen and twenty-one or twenty-two, depending on the course. They have consequently spent most of their life in a school environment that is normally teacher-orientated. It seems a little impractical to expect new undergraduates therefore to possess automatically the qualities needed to work and learn independently of the teacher. Furthermore, many students undertake undergraduate courses that are very different to anything they studied at school and will probably need a certain degree of focus to understand what exactly they are studying. For someone studying these courses or even courses that are essentially an extension of previous studies at school or in further education, it may be quite difficult to ascertain whether he is focused and therefore whether he is actually learning or is just frittering away his own time. Likewise, postgraduate students are each assigned to a supervisor who will monitor their progress and give them guidance and focus.

The exclusive adoption of either learning approach is neither desirable nor effective. Students need to be directed and helped in their learning, and the behaviourist approach seems to offer teachers the best method of monitoring student progress since some students will require more guidance than others. At the same time, however, constructivism allows the students to feel part of the learning process, which, in turn, can enhance their motivation. Over-reliance on either approach, though, can inhibit student learning because it may either stifle potential or give students too much freedom (allowing them to become lost and to lose focus). As a result, therefore, the most effective approach to learning is one that will both give students guidance and support when needed and also will encourage independent learning: in other words, an approach that includes both constructivism and behaviourism.

Learning environments: facilitators of learning

Whichever approach to learning is adopted, a learning environment will facilitate it. According to Hannafin and Land (1997: 194), there are four main elements of a learning environment: tools, resources, people and designs.

Tools

An environment requires the necessary implements to make it function. Tools could really include any form of material that is used to aid learning. In a classroom, for example, the blackboard (or whiteboard), overhead projector, chalk and pens, etc., are all used to help in the class delivery: these are all examples of tools in an environment.

Resources

Resources are needed to provide material for the learner to study and, according to Chase, 'a competent learning environment must contain information that is relevant to the interests and needs of its users' (1974: 286). Once again, in the traditional classroom scenario, if a teacher does not have books or other sources with information on a topic or activities for the students to undertake, this will hamper the teacher's efforts to prepare classes and give students material to study. The 'Master Classrooms project' at the University of North Carolina, Chapel Hill, illustrates this (Conway 1999: 3). Here, a series of thirteen classrooms have been built or traditional rooms converted into technology-enhanced classrooms where students and staff have access to computers, with links to the Internet. Computers are also connected to data projectors and similar equipment; all this offers a considerable technological landscape within which learning and teaching can occur. The design of these classrooms offers a wide range of tools and facilities to both teacher and learner. These features, in turn, can be used as appropriate by both student and teacher to access resources and ultimately therefore to develop student learning. The project provides an infrastructure for learning activity, containing tools and access to resources for learning. Nevertheless, if learning resources are unavailable in the first instance, the opportunities for learning will be more limited.

People

These are the users of the environment. The main objective of a learning environment is, after all, to facilitate learning and this requires human involvement. According to James Leed (1995: 15), a learning environment involves interaction between the learner and the teacher. Consequently, a learning environment needs to be designed with both groups in mind, with the ultimate goal of being pedagogically beneficial to the learner. As discussed earlier, the most effective way of achieving this is through the use of both constructivist and behaviourist learning approaches.

Environmental design

It does not seem adequate to design and provide an outer shell with the tools and resources necessary to gather and process information if no thought has been given to how these components will be used. As a result, the design of an environment extends beyond providing a physical background and towards the provision of relevant tools and resources, in addition to ensuring effective communication between the people who will use the environment.

In order to ensure that all aspects of an environment interact together, an infrastructure that will facilitate the distribution of information or resources to a specified destination is required (Harris, 1999: 141–42). If, for example, a tutor wishes to convey information to a class, he needs to use an effective means of communicating with his students. Communication of information cannot always take place within a designated teaching hour, for some students may not be present.

The boundaries of a learning environment

Iles believes that much learning 'occurs without the benefit of formal classroom training' (1994: 3). Although referring to learning by trial and error and, more specifically how a young child learns many skills in that way, he makes the very important point that a learning environment will not refer exclusively to the classroom environment. Schools and universities are examples of how a learning environment stretches beyond the classroom. Each one of them incorporates the four fundamental elements of a learning environment, discussed by Hannafin and Land (1997: 194): in the case of a school, there are people – the teachers and the taught – and resources such as books. Tools such as blackboards, pens and pencils are used to aid the process of learning. Schools and universities are specifically designed: there are specially equipped laboratories for science experiments to take place, technology and computer suites and even gymnasia, all of which allow students to practise certain activities and acquire certain skills. In both settings, however, the learning task does not stop outside the classroom. At universities, lectures and seminars provide students with the opportunity to gather information and act as a stimulus, encouraging them to think about ideas and concepts that have been presented to them. It is up to the student to then process this information for an essay, presentation or examination. This implies that since learning does not stop functioning when a lecture or seminar ends, the learning environment does not stop serving the student.

The role of language-learning environment

Language learning has undergone significant change over the past half century. The content of many degree programmes has evolved to incorporate significant emphasis on the communicative importance of language. Despite the changes, studying languages at specialist university level consists of two main stages: the study of the rules of language usage and application of language.

Rules of language usage

Inherent in the mastery of all four language-learning skills is the ability to construct coherent and accurate sentences, using an appropriate level of vocabulary and register: in other words, the ability to understand the rules of the language. This is learned both explicitly (through the learning of grammar rules and lists of vocabulary) and implicitly (the students learn through completing exercises, like translation or close activities, where they see sentence structure or new idiom being used).

There have been various discussions on the most appropriate method of teaching how to use the language (Adamson 1998: 170–183). Not surprisingly, there is a real danger that teaching grammar explicitly can cause students to lose interest; learning of lists of vocabulary or grammatical theory without seeing their usage in context may become very dense. The implicit approach places more responsibility for learning on the learner and may work for the more advanced and able learners, but those who need guidance and prompting from a teacher or other source of reference may struggle in that situation. Davies and Williams, quoting a study by Manning (1996), discovered that the implicit teaching of grammar was more beneficial for the learner, except when the students were confronted with difficult grammatical points (Davies and Williams 1998: 10). As a result, a combination of both approaches offers both flexibility and direction to the learner.

Language in use

This involves using target language as a means to an end, rather than an end in itself. The now ubiquitous study abroad aspect of most modern language degree programmes is a good example of this, where the target language is really used as a means of survival. Students need to use it to make purchases, pay bills or perform bank transactions, and other necessary tasks.

Other examples are the study of foreign language literature and area studies through the target language and tandem learning, which involves collaborative target-based learning, where the target language is used as a means of exchanging ideas or working on a project (Calvert 1992: 17).

Towards a language-learning environment

Unlike other areas of study in the field of humanities and arts, the two-stage process to language learning makes it quite unique. The way in which the first stage is linked to the second will have an impact on the way students ultimately use the language: either as an end in itself or as a means to an end (Scinicariello 1997: 189). In this regard, the role of the learning environment is significant.

Integration is required to enable the acquisition of the four skills of reading, writing, listening and speaking. Clearly, the acquisition of these skills implies the possession of others: writing requires the ability to read, while speaking requires the ability to listen. Many language activities integrate skills: translation and textual analysis activities, for example, integrate reading and writing skills; oral communication enhances listening and speaking skills.

Furthermore, the learner has an active role to play in the acquisition of the target language. King, Staczek and Tolzman (1998: 14) have described learner interaction and participation as fundamental traits of language learning and teaching. Interaction and participation in class provides practical experience for actively using the target language. This means that language learning and teaching are social activities. Since social learning activities often afford the learner neither the opportunity nor the time to digest and understand what is being taught (understanding grammatical principles is a good example), the learner also needs to work outside the social context, usually through private study.

The need to integrate learners, teachers, and learning activities makes the learning environment particularly relevant in the study of languages. A learning environment provides synergy among those involved in the learning process. If well designed, it offers an infrastructure to access resources, disseminate information and enable communication between learners and teachers inside and outside the classroom. In other words, it clearly enhances the process of learning. What is less clear, however, is the impact that computer technology has upon the role of the environment in enriching learning.

Chapter Two
Towards a computer-based environment

It has already been established that there are four main elements of any learning environment: tools, resources, people and designs (Hannafin and Land 1997: 194). In a computer-based environment, technology is integrated into each of the above elements. In other words, in such an environment, the computer will act as an aid to the learning process, facilitate learning through the provision of learning materials and resources and enable interaction between all learners and teachers involved in the environment. In addition, technology will be used in the creation of the environment's infrastructure, which links together the other three elements. The computer's role in these areas will be discussed below, firstly looking at its function within a generic environment, and then considering the role of such technology in a language-learning environment.

The computer as a learning aid

Since the early seventies, computer technology has been used to facilitate behaviourist and constructivist forms of learning. Generic and specialised Computer-Assisted Learning (CAL) software have been used to enhance the learning capabilities of students in many areas of study, including language learning.

The word processor as an aid to learner development

Word processing packages have been used in primary education, for example, as a means of encouraging young learners to express them-

29

selves and their ideas uninhibitedly. Dunn and Morgan (1987: 48–9) believe that word processing gives young learners the opportunity to participate willingly and enthusiastically in the production of written material for it offers the possibility of separating the technical skills of handwriting from the process of producing ideas on paper. They cite evidence that bad handwriting and the difficulty of forming correctly shaped letters can be very demoralising for some young learners and that the computer offers them a way of expressing their ideas without feeling discouraged by the difficulties of writing (Dunn and Morgan 1984: 48–9). Likewise, the word processor allows the learner to type a first draft and then to correct spelling or alter punctuation. These are problematic areas for young children who are just beginning to learn about the intricacies of their mother language. Many adults can also sympathise with some problems of punctuation, such as the ubiquitous comma or the overused apostrophe.

Computer-Assisted Learning (CAL) programs

Schools and universities use specially designed programs to aid student learning. One notable example of these CAL packages is *Logo*, designed by Seymour Papert, which is still used by school children today. This program, mainly used for mathematical experiments, is a form of programming language for young children. The young learners type a series of instructions on a computer, for example, a series of commands to draw a flower or a bird and then *Logo* draws the object, using these instructions. According to Davy (1984: 11), this package allows young children to think like a computer and so learn to think mechanically. When it was created, *Logo* was seen as a way of using a machine mainly used by adults (the computer) to teach young children important mathematical skills. It simulates many children's activities, such as drawing flowers or animals, yet requires the children to think in quite a mature way in order to programme the drawing instructions on to a computer (Davy 1984: 15). The *Logo* program, which was created in 1980, is actually an example of constructivist learning since the learner (in this case, the young child) inputs the necessary information to make the program draw a shape: if

30

the child enters the wrong command, the program will not draw the item correctly and so the young learner must change the erroneous command and try again and continue trying until the program has drawn the correct shape. This method of trial and error shows one of the early uses of computer technology as a means of letting children learn autonomously.

CAL programs are also used as tutoring systems. *Logo* is an example of the computer taking on the role of tutee, where essentially the learner is in control of the learning activity. Other CAL packages use behaviourist learning techniques to teach ideas or concepts. The use of drill and practice exercises which take the learner from one level to the next upon successful completion of the previous level are an example. This means that if the learner does not complete a particular level successfully, he may not be able to move on to the next stage until he has attempted the current level again and attained a satisfactory number of correct answers.

Another example of constructivist computer-based learning is the use of computer technology to simulate experiments, thereby allowing the learner to apply theory to practice. Wojciech Grega, from the Technical University of Mining and Metallurgy at Krakow, Poland has documented many of these computer-based experiments (1995: 517–30). One of these includes an interface between a computer terminal and a helicopter rotor that operates when data is fed into the computer and variables are set. The computer is used as a means of demonstrating an experiment and controlling it. If the variables are changed, the speed and direction of the helicopter blade will be affected. In this scenario, the computer takes on the role of a simulator, where it operates the rotor, and allows students to change the variables that will affect the speed and direction of the rotor. Using the computer to control a helicopter rotor is more realistic than using a real helicopter and offers an authentic context for the learners, which, as described in the previous chapter, represents an important trait of a learning environment.

The most common way that computer technology has been used as an aid to language learning has been through the use of specially designed learning programs known as computer-assisted language learning programs (CALL). Extensive interest in these packages developed in the early eighties (Levy 1997: 22). CALL programs perform two main roles.

Firstly, they are used as a tutor, adopting the role of the teacher. In other words, the students select suitable answers to activity-based questions and the program indicates whether the answers are correct (Yazdani 1986: 145). Many of the early CALL exercises were drill and practice activities, often focusing on the study of grammar (Paramskas 1993: 124 and Levy 1997: 102). There are, of course, CALL tutoring systems that focus on other areas of language learning. A recent program, developed at the University of Warwick, is designed to teach ESL students how to listen to lectures given in English, which is their target language.[1] This program, based on CD-ROM, exposes learners to a number of different video clips of lectures delivered in English on a wide variety of different topics. Students must then respond to questions based on each clip. Students will work through each stage of the program: there are over thirty hours of material to be worked through. Through constant practice, answering questions and summarising important points from lectures, the program helps the ESL students to maximise their understanding of lectures given in the target language. This type of package, aside from training the student how to listen to a foreign language, which enhances aural skills, also provides the user with exposure to authentic target language grammar and idiom.

CALL software are also used as a tool to develop course materials. Examples include authoring packages, such as *Hypercard, Authorware, Storyboard*, and *CAN-8*. They provide a shell around which the teacher adds course or class-specific language material or exercises to be used by students, often including graphics, hyperlinks and

[1]   Program demonstrated at EUROCALL 2000, Dundee.

sound. In some cases, these authoring programs are used to present class material or exercises in a more stimulating way to engage the interest of the students. *Wordstore*, for example, allows users to record vocabulary in a categorised dictionary, giving users both the opportunity to organise vocabulary effectively and to retrieve words or phrases with greater ease when completing a translation or other similar text (Jones 1986: 176). Other packages used to simplify normal class activities include concordance programs that monitor word or phrase usage in a text. The University of Ulster, for example, uses concordance software, as part of the *TAP* (Textual Analysis Program), to facilitate textual analysis and to pinpoint grammatical structures within a passage.

Whereas the effectiveness of CALL software is the subject of continuous research as developments and improvements to packages are ongoing, it is widely recognised that CALL has two notable advantages. Firstly, Sciarone and Meijer (1993: 95) argue that CALL programs can be used for quite tedious tasks such as teaching grammar and vocabulary acquisition, providing students with appropriate grammar practice exercises and feedback. Since learning grammar often involves continual practice, it would require considerable time commitment from staff to correct and assess all practice exercises. CALL programs will never tire, unlike the human teacher, and can be used repeatedly (Powell 1998: 186). Some CALL packages can carry out all the assessment, which means that the teacher does not have to be present to assess these exercises and, as a result, students can use CALL outside the classroom, in areas of self-study, for example. Students can therefore work at their own speed (Allan 1990: 73). This allows constructivist learning to take place: students can use CALL packages for remedial work or revision of problematic grammar or similar topics, in their own time. One of the characteristics of constructivism is that the teacher is not excluded from the learning process and CALL can be used to retain the teacher's involvement in the learning process. When students use CALL packages for grammar practice or similar areas of language learning, for example, the teacher therefore has more time to devote to preparing other types of classes, engage in research or enjoy more meaningful contact time with students, concentrating on specific problems that they may have, oral fluency or essay or translation technique, for example. At the Queen's University of Belfast, students in first year French classes are required to use the in-house *Prof* grammar program in their own time to learn grammar, with a written class test at the end of the semester. This replaces the need to timetable systematic grammar classes each week and frees up the teacher in charge for other tasks.

In addition, CALL has a certain edutainment value. Many modern programs make effective use of graphics and colour and recorded sound: they are therefore eye-catching. Some CALL programs, like *Tesoros*, are game-based.[2] The generation of students that uses these programs has grown up in a computer-game culture and can therefore feel an affinity with the game-based activities of some CALL packages. This has obvious academic value, since students can be attracted to the programs that teach often tedious aspects of grammar and vocabulary. Even some critics of CALL programs have accepted their motivational value (Ross 1991: 65). The real test for these programs is that often students will return to use them repeatedly in their own time, in areas of self-study, for example, in spite of the seemingly tedious areas of language learning that they address. If this were not so, there would be little need nor justification for creating self-access CALL areas, yet many universities have them in place and others are creating such a facility.

CALL is however not a panacea for language learning and has considerable limitations. Graham Davies points out, in his recent article on the history of CALL, that these programs are not suitably spontaneous (2000). In other words, they do not yet have the ability to react to the unforeseen. Therefore, whereas they may be very useful for giving students endless opportunities to practise grammar or vocabulary exercises and give immediate feedback on the correctness of the answer without the presence of a teacher, if students do not understand the mistakes they make, the help sections that many CALL

2   *Tesoros* is an introductory Spanish program that teaches grammar and vocabulary within the context of a mystery adventure published by McGraw-Hill Education.

packages provide are limited by the information that the programmer has fed into the help section database. They cannot address questions that have not been pre-programmed. In spite of considerable efforts to create Intelligent Computer-Assisted Language Learning (ICALL) systems that will have Artificial Intelligence and will respond spontaneously and answer questions just as a human teacher would, these systems are still very limited.[3] It appears that CALL systems have insufficient technological capability to recognise and respond to the human voice (Ehsani and Knodt 1998: 45–60). One of the most spontaneous and least mechanical areas of language learning is oral work (and its mastery is important if the learner intends to use the foreign language as a means of communication with native speakers, for example). Students cannot yet conduct a conversation in a foreign language with a computer: human contact is required for this type of interaction.[4]

Computer-Assisted Language-Learning programs have suffered the wrath of teacher misconception. In its role as a tutor, CALL has been seen as a replacement to the human teacher. Jones (1983: 171) describes how the early history of CALL was concerned with using it as a substitute for the teacher. In other words, CALL meant redundancy for the teacher; at least that is how many teachers perceived it. They began to think that if they encouraged or used CALL, before long, they would have little or no role in teaching students. As a result, these teachers would not use CALL, fearing for their own positions within languages departments and, in turn, would remain oblivious to the possibilities for using CALL. The myth surrounding CALL still exists, although CALL researchers are engaged in a continuous battle to change this perception. Levy, for example, argues that it is important for language teachers to have a more direct role in the production of CALL software, thereby ensuring the pedagogical relevance of these programs. Furthermore, he argues that, far from

---

3   The Athena Language-Learning Project at MIT is currently developing learning software that uses Artificial Intelligence.

4   See Levy (2000: 182) for further discussion on the value of face-to-face contact over computer-mediated interaction.

making teachers redundant, the advent of CALL programs requires them to guide students in the use of such software to ensure maximal educational benefit (Levy 1997: 231).

Integrating CALL into the language-learning environment

CALL programs have an important academic role: they can assist the process of grammar and vocabulary acquisition that were described in the previous chapter as crucial aspects of language learning. In other activities, such as translation or textual analysis, they represent a very useful tool. However, as both Levy (1997: 24) and Jones (1986: 171) argue, CALL programs need to be used in an appropriate context and not as stand-alone creations. This suggests that CALL programs need to be used as part of the language-learning environment, used alongside other teaching methods and resources, such as books and oral exercises.

How is this achieved? Integration into the languages curriculum is required (Levy 1997: 226). In other words, rather than just being used for self-study or as a replacement for normal classes that teach grammar and vocabulary, CALL will be used as an integral part of those classes. Since CALL lacks the spontaneity of a teacher, it is ill equipped to explain grammatical theory in the same way as a human tutor. The *Prof* program illustrates this: the program cannot tell a student why he or she has given the wrong answer to a grammar question because this information is not programmed into the package. Instead, the student is advised to return to the grammar theory section at the start of the lesson. In this scenario, it is quite feasible that the student might simply not understand the grammatical explanation given by the program: the teacher, on the other hand, can explain the theory further and use language and examples that the student can relate to. A more effective approach may be to leave the explanation of grammar theory to the human teacher and encourage students to use CALL packages to test out their understanding of the grammar. The instant feedback provided by such packages would allow students to recognize areas of grammar that they have not yet grasped or possibly allow the teacher to quickly become aware of grammar areas that need more explanation. Students may then seek further explanation from the teacher: this would allow the teacher to focus on specific areas of grammar and deal with precise grammar deficiencies. Likewise, the teacher would not need to correct hundreds of grammar exercises, spending considerable time doing so, to show students which areas of grammar need further study: some CALL programs print off score sheets for each exercise, listing mistakes made or showing which answers are wrong, offering instant feedback to students. The teacher could collect these score sheets, or ask students to assess their own performance, in order to become aware of which areas of grammar need more attention in class. Using CALL grammar packages in this way would employ both the machine and the human tutor in an integrated way that, rather than portraying both as rivals which replace each other's work, gives both an important role in helping the student and allows for maximal staff-student contact time.

Students in self-study areas may work on areas of language not dealt with in class –certain grammar topics or a more extensive range of aural exercises, for example. Using a system like *CAN-8* or *Robotel*, the instructor can monitor student progress from a remote computer workstation and quickly become aware of areas of student deficiency that may require remedial work in class time.

The integration of other CALL packages into the language-learning environment is also possible. Several translation tools, like *TransIT Tiger* and *MetaText* (produced for the TELL Consortium), provide a framework around which translation activities can be organised. *TransIT Tiger*, for example, gives students access to model translations that can be used to provide invaluable tips on translation technique (Talbot 1996: 20–3). *MetaText* provides a hyperlinked electronic notebook to help the student work on translating texts and consult categorised databanks of vocabulary and grammar (Gillespie 1994: 143). A common feature in each of the examples mentioned above is that the use of CALL for self-study is earthed into class activity and mainstream teaching to ensure curriculum relevance: an idea suggested by Gillespie (1995: 154).

The Computer as a resource

Computer technology has been used as a resource to help student learning for nearly thirty years. It has been used both in generic learning contexts and specifically for language learning.

The use of databases to archive reference material is a good example of its generic use. University libraries use database applications to log details of the books and articles that they hold. These electronic catalogues allow students quicker access to material in the library. Instead of flicking through the pages of paper-based catalogues, the user can access details of the works of a particular author or works dealing with a certain topic that are held by the library almost instantaneously. Some libraries offer on-line reservation and book renewal facilities, which mean that students can reserve a book, or renew a loan on a book from a networked computer terminal within the university or even from a computer in another country if the library facilities are accessible over the Web. One of the first electronic catalogues, at least in the UK, was created by the New University of Ulster (now the University of Ulster) in 1975 (Wintour and McDowell 1976: 61). The system was initially used to log details of new books and journals in the library and to keep track of outstanding loans.

In more recent times, the Internet has become a major source of reference for students. The World Wide Web, for example, is used by many university courses to provide students with resources such as lecture notes. The School of History, Philosophy and Politics at the University of Ulster has set up a password-protected Web gateway to lecture notes and tutorial information, available to undergraduate students of History. Tutors on the course can use an electronic noticeboard to send information to students and receive comments from them. This Web experiment is still in its infancy and students are only beginning to learn about it and use it. In fact, according to the project co-ordinator, the notes and coursework information serve as a window for potential students considering a course of study in

History, showing the kind of material and workload that they can expect from studying that course.

A similar example is the School of Pharmacy in the University of Brighton. Here, students access the Pharmacy Intranet – an internal network in which each course or module has its own Web page. Students use these pages to download copies of lecture transparencies, past examination papers and access other similar resources (Grega and Doughty 1995: 517–30). These resources however supplement much of the work done in class and do not replace class interaction.[5] Students still attend classes, carry out experiments and interact with each other and members of staff. If they miss points made in a lecture, they can download notes from the Intranet. These notes are copies of the transparencies used in the lecture and therefore contain the key points covered and are not verbatim transcripts of everything mentioned in the lecture. Consequently, any students who rely solely on these electronic notes for examination or coursework preparation, rather than attending the lectures, would find considerable gaps in that information.

In addition to being used as a pedagogical resource, students and staff use computer technology as an administrative resource, too. Databases, containing hours and locations of classes are used when compiling timetables in schools and universities. Examination results are now published on the Web in many institutions (using secure authentication). This type of system gives students global access to resources and material that formerly could only be accessed on campus: in other words, the boundaries of the teaching and learning environment are changing.

5   This view was supported by the results of a questionnaire, carried out among staff in the School of Pharmacy. 68% of respondents believed that the computer resources should mainly supplement their teaching (N=28).

Although often used synonymously with the Internet, the World Wide Web (WWW) is a means of browsing information stored on the different networks across the Internet. According to Haworth (1996: 173), the Internet existed ten years before the WWW was created. The Web has been described as 'the world's largest database' (Haworth 1996: 175). There is a wide range of material available: in 2002, there are approximately 800 million pages on the Web.[6] Haworth has divided the material into two categories: uni-directional and bi-directional material (1996: 174). The first category includes material that the user cannot interact with: read-only material. The second category is interactive.

Uni-directional material includes on-line magazines and newspapers and cultural information, such as websites of political parties, information about regions in the target language country. On-line newspapers in the target language are very valuable to the learner: they are written in the target language for a native audience and are therefore truly authentic language material, which are useful to enhance reading skills. Furthermore, they expose the learners to a wealth of native writing skills, and the more assiduous learners will use this to improve their own writing skills in the target language. The information they provide is also very significant: Levy (1997: 95) explains how they provide up-to-date news and therefore allow the learner to keep well informed about developments in the target language country. At present, many university libraries subscribe to target language newspapers, such as *Le Figaro* and *El Mundo*, receiving regular consignments of hard copies of these newspapers. The main disadvantage of this arrangement is that there is often a time delay, of at least one day, between publication of the papers and their arrival in the university libraries. The Web reduces this time delay: language students and teachers can access newspapers articles the day that they are published, a luxury usually only available to those who

---

6   Results from the NEC Research Institute, accessed on WWW, May 2002: http://www.internetindicators.com/facts.html

live in the target language country. Whereas some on-line newspapers are now only available to paying subscribers, a number of are free, giving students and staff an additional incentive to use the on-line.

Other media sources are available over the Web. An increasing number of radio stations broadcast over the Web and some television channels like France 3, M6 and TF1 broadcast video clips of news reports on the WWW. The quality of these broadcasts varies, depending on the university network speed or Web traffic, however even on a low speed network, audio quality is fairly high. The potential for this type of material is obvious. Some broadcasts are live; others are pre-recorded and can be played, paused and rewound using applications like *Windows Media Player* or *RealPlayer*. As a result, teachers may use pre-recorded broadcasts in class-based aural activities, such as listening comprehension, either in a computer lab or in a classroom where all students have networked laptops. Equally, students can use this type of audio and video material, both pre-recorded and live, for independent study.

Language learners use the Web to access other material relating to the target language country. For students of Area Studies, the Web is used to find up-to-date information about political parties and policies in the target language country, as well as facts about regions and towns in that country. Some governments provide downloadable versions of new legislation or speeches made by political leaders. Students of ESL especially will find a plethora of information about North American politics, including political speeches, such as the President's State of the Union address.

The Web contains a great deal of interactive material. CALL programs are available over the Web. The WELL (Web-Enhanced Language Learning) project, for example, provides links to several on-line language learning exercises in a number of different languages for beginners, intermediate and advanced learners. Many other on-line exercises are created as part of CALL research projects. In addition, the Web offers a range of on-line dictionaries, some of which are also research projects like the University of Chicago's ARTFL French-English Dictionary.[7]

An increasing number of programs can be downloaded across the Web. Just as the advent of the CD saw a paradigm shift in the way CALL programs were stored, hence affecting the multimedia capabilities of the programs, the Web increases the portability of CALL packages because they can be directly downloaded, through the browser, to a local machine. At the moment, a number of CALL programs are downloadable through the websites of CALL publishers like Camosoft and WIDA.

The Web offers many advantages to the learner and teacher. By providing up-to-date information and articles, accessible from any Internet-linked machine, students and staff can use the Web at home or on campus, giving twenty-four hour access to these materials, something that is not possible with conventional university library resources. This gives tutors the opportunity to prepare lessons, using Web material like newspaper articles, whilst at home in the evenings. Similarly, students are free to browse the Web for material, read newspaper articles or use CALL packages in their own time.

Gillespie and McKee (1999b: 445) found that students used the Web for independent study at the University of Ulster more often than they would use CALL programs. This can be explained by the attractive interface provided by the Web. Burgess and Eastman (1997: 163) explain that the Web is 'sexy' in computing terms: students find Web-based newspapers more exciting and dynamic than 'paper' equivalents.

In this context, the Web is a valuable resource for constructivist learning. One of the key characteristics of this approach to learning is that learner plays an active role in the process of knowledge building. The Web encourages students to navigate around it in their own way and disseminate appropriate information (Burgess and Eastman 1997: 164). Teachers may set assignments that require students to search the

---

7   Part of the ARTFL (American and French Research on the Treasury of the French Language) project. Accessed on the World Wide Web, January 2001: http://humanities.uchicago.edu/ARTFL.html

Web to find the answers, for example. It is a way of linking the language classroom to the outside world, providing access to a gamut of resources, exercises and material that are available worldwide. Often, many of the sites that they will be searching will be written in the target language and the ability to navigate their way successfully around these websites gives them authentic exposure to the target language. In their analysis of the value of the Web, Burgess and Eastman conclude that it is a valuable language learning resource because 'anything that motivates students to be willing to be confronted by the foreign language is to be welcomed' (Burgess and Eastman 1997: 165).

Integration into a language-learning environment: overcoming the limitations of the World Wide Web

It is important to recognise that the Web is only part of a language-learning environment. Conacher and Royall confirm that on its own, it is just a tool; the way that it is used however can make a difference to teaching and learning (Conacher and Royall 1998: 41).

Before encouraging students to use the Web profusely and thereby swamping them with too much material, it is necessary to establish some kind of structure to the Web. Haworth (1996: 180) points out that the Web is not coherently organised. Search engines are used to locate websites, however since new sites appear continually, the engines must be updated constantly and there is currently no universally perfect search engine. Often the user will have to spend considerable time searching for the desired information, which is a source of demotivation. Felix (1999: 31) points out that another problem with search engines is that although they can be used to pinpoint language-learning sites, they do not (or cannot) evaluate how good the resources offered by such sites are. Similarly, the Web is not yet controlled by a regulatory presiding authority: anyone is free to publish anything on a website and is not restrained by the protocol that is used in printed media. The contents of some pages may be of dubious origin, even plagiarised. The unsuspecting student, unaware of this lack of regulatory control, may download material and use it in an essay or other piece of work, thinking it is accurate because it has been published on the Web. In fact, the opposite may be true: some material ends up on the Web because publishers do not accept it. Bel and Ingraham (1997: 108) believe that, in view of the wealth of spurious material (and accurate, but unstructured information), tutors have a responsibility to guide students when they browse the Web, recommending sites that they have visited and confirming their accuracy.

The same is true for on-line dictionaries and CALL packages. Some dictionaries are very limited in content. This is understandable because there would be little point selling dictionaries like the *Le Grand Robert*, if the same voluminous editions could be accessed on-line, free of charge. Equally, some on-line CALL exercises are aimed at very basic level linguists and not university students in their second or third year of a languages degree (Haworth 1996: 176–77). Tutors have a responsibility to guide students away from unsuitable material and towards material appropriate to their level. One way of directing students through the Web is to create a Web gateway. This is a structured platform, which provides links to different websites that may be divided into categories according to language or content, for example links to on-line dictionaries, CALL packages (both Web and CD/LAN based) and historical or cultural sites. A gateway makes it much easier for students to find websites, instead of using a plethora of search engines. An effective gateway will provide links that are highly relevant to students' courses of study – consequently the creation of such gateways is probably best left to course tutors, who have a thorough understanding of the requirements of their language curriculum. In addition, given the ephemeral nature of the World Wide Web, with new pages and users appearing every day, the tutors will be engaged in the continual task of monitoring the Web for material that would be useful for their students and updating gateways.

There are also some technical problems with the WWW. Slow data transmission speeds means that information is not always accessible. Accessing information on the Web using a modem (students or staff may be likely to do so from their own computer at home in the evenings) can be a tiresome process. Low data transmission speeds are particularly problematic when downloading pages with graphics, sound files or video clips – the types of files that are used in CALL programs and by on-line radio and television stations. If the connection is not a problem, there may be a server outage or it may not have the capacity to allow access to multiple users simultaneously. All these factors can conspire to make the Web seem more of an obstacle than a benefit to the learner. These problems may be solved in the future, making the Web more reliable.

The resources that the Web offers and the access to target language textual and audiovisual material provide unquestionable support to the language learning process (Felix 1999: 36). Although the dubious nature of some material is problematic, it could be argued that if it is written in the target language, it still exposes students to authentic language, therefore helping to enhance their reading and writing skills. The technical problems associated with it at the moment mean that it is not a perfect language learning resource, but there can be problems with printed material too: books may not be available in the library or out of print (Orlandi 1999: 56). The World Wide Web has an important role in a language-learning environment, but the human tutor has a role to play to ensure that it is used effectively and it seems apposite to avoid considering the Web as a panacea, but rather as a useful aid to learner and teacher.

The Computer as a resource

The third feature of a learning environment is the level of interaction between those who use the environment. In reality, this means facilitating communication between users. Computer technology is used for this purpose in two main areas: as a means of presenting work and to enable general communication between staff and students

Word processing software allows staff and students to prepare work and material in a clearly legible, neat and coherent format. Other presentational packages integrate word processing functions with graphical manipulation (*MS Publisher* and *PowerPoint* are examples). PowerPoint, in particular is useful for preparing overhead slides. Unlike OHPs, however, PowerPoint and similar packages allow teachers to design impressive slide presentations, incorporating graphics, sound and attractive fonts, and display them from a CPU or laptop connected to a data projector, without the need to print off hard copies. These types of packages have led to improvements in the way that staff and students communicate information and ideas to one another.

The word processor is useful, too, for communicating with physically handicapped learners, such as the blind. At the beginning of the eighties, several word processing systems were designed for this purpose. One example was the Learning and Working Environment for the Blind (LWEB). This system would translate word processed text material into Braille, which meant that a teacher of sighted students did not need to prepare a text specifically for blind students in the class (Schweikhardt 1981: 463). Likewise, the blind student could compose work, using a Braille keyboard, and the program would translate this into ordinary text, enabling the work to be read by his sighted teacher. LWEB also included a calculator for the blind as well as a graphics program that allowed the blind student to draw on the computer screen by typing some commands onto the computer keyboard. LWEB therefore allowed blind students to be taught in the same class as students with sight.

Computer-Mediated Communication (CMC)

Telecommunication networks are examples of how the computer is used for more direct communication. Networks have proved valuable in linking various computers to each other and allow information to be exchanged between them. The proliferation of the Internet has led to considerable improvements in the way computers are used across the world for communication. In 1996, library staff in secondary schools in the East Baton Rouge Parish district of Louisiana started an Internet-based project (Taylor and Dupuis 1995: 704–11). Schools in this area were in a poor economic situation and their textual resources were becoming dated; their ability to acquire new resources was very limited. Librarians in several secondary schools pooled their efforts to set up the Web in their schools and jointly search the Internet for material that would be of educational use in their libraries. A local network linked all the schools, and librarians used internal e-mail to communicate with one another and share details of sites of common interest. The results of that project were encouraging: more funding and technical support was made available for the project the following year to facilitate public access to these resources across the Internet (Taylor and Dupuis 1995: 708). This example demonstrates that one of the main advantages of the Internet (especially e-mail) is that it allows for quick and efficient communication for users who may be separated by distance or time. This allows students and staff to send and receive coursework off-campus. Electronic submission of work is particularly useful for distance learning courses and when it is impractical to attend campus, such as at weekends or late the evening when the campus is closed.

Use within a language-learning environment

In addition to the many uses of these packages in the generic environment, they all offer a further advantage in the language-learning context. In the case of word processing, some programs offer a split screen facility that is useful for comparing a text typed in different languages (Brierley and Kemble 1991: 14). The search facility allows the user to calculate the number of occurrences of certain words in a text. In an essay, this facility can help improve the style of the work by encouraging the user to replace overused words or expressions with appropriate synonyms (Brierley and Kemble 1991: 14).

An increasing number of word processing packages provide built-in dictionaries. This is the case with *MS Word 2000* (as part of the *MS Office* suite), which has a number of pre-installed dictionaries and will automatically detect the language that the user is typing and change the dictionary settings to that language. These dictionaries and grammar checkers are becoming increasingly comprehensive (Garrett 1991: 84). The improved quality of spelling and grammar checkers available at present raises questions over the ethics of using such facilities. Does it not encourage students to become indolent when typing the foreign language? Do they really need to check over each word if the computer program will do it for them? This is, of course, a potential problem that may perhaps be remedied through rigorous class testing, where students do not have access to spelling or grammar checkers.

Whereas these checkers are useful for fixing annoying typos, which are not necessarily caused by linguistic incompetence but rather by a simple typing error, they are not totally flawless. English spell checkers challenge the spelling of words that are particularly technical or that have not been pre-programmed into the dictionary database, even if they are spelt correctly. The same is true for foreign language dictionaries. Grammar checkers, although useful, sometimes make syntactical changes that change the meaning of sentences and do not always correct typos like 'they' instead of 'the'. Given the varied writing styles and forms of expression, grammar and spell checkers that could cope effectively with all aspects of language would need access to huge databanks, that would either take many years to produce or would use vast amounts of hard disk space: such databanks may not even be commercially viable to create. Perhaps it will not be until the arrival of fully functioning artificial intelligence that grammar and spelling checkers will become totally reliable. In the interim, using spelling and grammar checkers will not be enough to ensure total syntactic accuracy or even coherency: the human checker is still required.

The use of computer-mediated communication tools within a language-learning environment is similar to its use within a generic context, although there are a number of ways that make the use of computer technology particularly pertinent for language learning. The proliferation of audiovisual and text-based forms of synchronous and asynchronous communication has brought a number of advantages to the language learner. Firstly, since e-mail is a very popular tool for students: many use it regularly to communicate with friends in other institutions. Students seem to enjoy communicating electronically: this is clearly supported by the explosion of a recent phenomenon: students use the now ubiquitous mobile telephone to 'text' friends (using SMS – Short Messaging Service) who are sometimes sitting at the other end of the classroom! Therefore, text-based electronic communication interests students: if they are encouraged to use it for academic purposes, its pedagogical value is considerable.

The asynchronous nature of e-mail and other forms of text-based communication allows students time to think about what they are reading and writing and therefore seems useful in developing two out of the four main language learning skills. In an oral conversation that is conducted in the speakers' native language, the interlocutors have limited time to think through what they are saying and formulate responses to each other's questions. If the conversation is conducted in the target language, the amount of thinking time required is increased, although the reaction time to questions is often the same as it would be in the native language. The task is all the more difficult for students whose fluency in the target language is not yet very high. Text-based communication is a useful way of encouraging these types of students to use the target language for communication and gain confidence in it (Kötter, Shield and Stevens 1999: 59). There is less pressure for immediate responses to questions asked over e-mail and the student can work at his own pace (Desmarais 1998: 324). Some students who are reluctant to speak in class in their native language, not to mention their target language, because they feel embarrassed, may prefer to use text-based communication. Woodin and Ojanguren (1997: 506) point out that e-mail (and other forms of text-based communication) offers a form of one-to-one communication that is not available in a classroom situation, where students are subjected to the implicit fear of making a fool of themselves in front of the rest of the class by asking a question that seems too ridiculous even to mention. If students who are naturally shy and would not normally speak in class, or have poor linguistic ability, feel encouraged to use text-based communication to communicate in the target language, this may improve their confidence in using the language, perhaps encouraging them to speak more regularly in class, and thereby improving their fluency in the language.

The benefits of text-based communication, along with obvious cost efficiency and speed explain why tandem projects often require partners to communicate by computer. The International Tandem Project is a good example, with participating students from many different countries. The project initially only involved three universities: Sheffield, Bochum and Oviedo with students taking part in exchange visits that were obviously costly. The proliferation of Internet communication, such as e-mail, throughout university campuses provided a cheaper infrastructure for tandem communication and saw a number of new universities joining the Project (Woodin and Ojanguren 1997: 488).

At the same time, however, it is questionable whether e-mail has a positive effect on written language. Biesenbach-Lucas and Weasenforth (2001: 156) did not find conclusive proof that e-mail is beneficial to students' academic writing. They demonstrated, however, that one of the dangers of e-mail is that it lacks the lexical cohesiveness of written or even word-processed work (Biesenbach-Lucas and Weasenforth, 2001: 137). Typing mistakes, word or sentence abbreviations and ellipses are very common in e-mail: this can be problematic for tandem or collaborative learning activities because, if a native speaker uses this type of mistake-ridden style of writing in e-mails, it is possible that his partner will copy the style. This is especially pernicious for learners whose linguistic standard is low anyway. On the other hand, students with a high linguistic level may find it useful to be exposed to that type of style to heighten their cultural awareness of the use of the target language and will be suitably competent to not replicate it in formal language use.

Asynchronous communication is an effective way of making contact when it is not practical to speak to the person directly. When both parties are separated by distance or other impediment, e-mail or computer conferencing allow the interlocutors to make contact. When students have problems or need assistance or guidance, it may not always be practical to speak to the tutors in person because of busy teaching schedules or because either party is not available on campus. Asynchronous communication is an effective solution to this problem.

Unlike a telephone conversation, both parties do not need to be on-line at the same time and so tutors will be able to reply to student queries when they have time or are not teaching. Gillespie and McKee (1999a: 44) and Levy (1997: 97) show that e-mail and other forms of asynchronous communication are an effective help-line for students.

Similarly, it is possible to use text-based communication to provide a synchronous link between tutor and student, in the form of a virtual chat. A student working from a computer at home or in a computer lab, for example, may be able to contact his tutor who working at a computer in his office at the same time, without having to leave the computer terminal.

Improvements in the speed and processing capabilities of computers have made it easier to use audiovisual conferencing. This has led to the creation of audiovisual forms of CMC that offer the type of spontaneous oral interpersonal communication that Garrett (1991: 80) did not consider possible through the medium of a computer. These include electronic video and audio mail and computer-based video/ audio conferencing. The advent of inexpensive webcams and sound recording equipment means that an increasing number of computer users can communicate audiovisually instead of through the medium of text. The implications for language learning are considerable.

Audiovisual communication is a useful link to tutors, just like e-mail and other forms of text-based CMC. Video conferencing has been used as a means of conducting classes when a face-to-face meeting is not possible. Goodfellow, Jeffreys, Miles and Shirra (1996: 8) used video conferencing to teach a course in Professional English, designed by the London School of English, for students at the Norwegian Insurance Academy. This can be particularly beneficial for universities where similar subject areas are taught on different campuses and staff travel between campuses to teach these subjects. This would effectively allow one tutor to give the same lecture or class simultaneously to students spread over different locations, reducing teaching or travelling costs. Classes may be given through audio conferencing, although the lack of visual contact means the loss of some non-verbal aspects of the spoken language (O'Dowd, 2000: 50). O'Dowd points out that ISDN video conferencing offers good quality and is suitable for the delivery of language classes (2000: 51).

ISDN technology is very expensive, often requiring dedicated connections and equipment and it is also costly to use. As a result, it is often impractical to have access to this form of video conferencing technology in every teaching room or even computer lab. On the other hand, computer-mediated video and audio conferencing is less expensive. It is possible to broadcast sound and video over the Web with relative ease and without major expense for the end user. The software and hardware required for computer-mediated conferencing is relatively inexpensive too. Some audio and video conferencing software packages are available on a free download. According to O'Dowd, computer-mediated video conferencing does not produce the same quality as ISDN because the bandwidth of Internet connections affects the projection rate of images, reducing its suitability as a tool for class delivery (2000: 51). This is true at present: some webcams and Internet connections cannot broadcast images at the accepted minimum projection rate of thirty frames per second and, as a result, pictures are often jerky and disjointed. The same is true for audio conferencing: sound transmission can be interrupted quite easily if the connection is not fast enough, although it is less problematic than video transmission because it requires less bandwidth than video conferencing. Nevertheless, the quality is improving all the time: higher resolution cameras are being produced and the speed of microprocessors improves all the time, leading to faster processing capabilities, better graphics and improved sound quality. Furthermore, network connections are becoming faster with many universities operating high-speed networks and affordable domestic broadband connections have become common.

Computer-mediated audio and video conferencing is particularly effective for one-to-one or small group links. Just like e-mail, they can be used to provide a help-line between tutor and student. It is sometimes easier to give help or guidance orally than through written instructions: computer-mediated video or audio conferencing provides the means for doing so. Since computer-mediated video and audio technology is relatively inexpensive, institutions may be in a financial position to equip entire computer labs or CALL labs with these facilities. Students will then be able to use video or audio conferencing to communicate with their tutors orally, perhaps to seek advice on matters that they feel unable to express in writing. This may be particularly advantageous when students are located on another campus from staff or are not within reasonable travelling distance, which would make it impractical to visit staff in person. In addition, this kind of oral communication can be conducted in the target language: unlike text-based communication in the target languages, students will not have the same time to think about what they want to say and will need to react more quickly. This may give them very valuable practice using the target language for oral communication. Another possibility is to use these forms of communication to link foreign language students with native speakers in the target language countries. This, in turn, gives the learners the opportunity to develop aural language learning skills, exposing them to accents and aspects of the spoken language that they normally would only encounter by visiting the target language country. If links are established between students of the target language and native speakers based in the region or area where the students intend to stay during their residence abroad, this can help them learn more about that area and establish friendships that may prove invaluable during their stay abroad. Such contact would be a useful component of tandem work. If used in addition to e-mail communication, it could provide yet another bond between tandem partners.

Whereas audiovisual computer-mediated communication tends to be conducted synchronously, there are some advantages using it for asynchronous communication. Audio and video messages can be sent as e-mail attachments: they obviously lack the same spontaneity as synchronous conferencing, but may be a useful alternative for tutors when synchronous contact is not possible. Likewise, some tutors may wish to give students oral instructions in the target language, essay topics or guidelines for example, rather than presenting them in a written format. This will expose students to aspects of the target language, such as accent and tone, which are not obvious in written language. Moreover, unlike video and audio conferencing, which is dependent on a satisfactory Internet connection, audio and video clips sent as e-mail attachments can be accessed offline and are not dependent on a fast connection.

Environmental infrastructure

In a computer-based environment, technology can be used to create infrastructure that will ensure the three remaining elements (tools, people and resources) interact with one another. One of the clearest illustrations of this is a Virtual Learning Environment (VLE). In this type of environment, students use the Web to access details of assignments, course outlines, multimedia resources, class lists, and electronic noticeboards as well as having the ability to e-mail work to tutors and receive feedback electronically. Many VLEs are created using computer software systems such as *TopClass* and *WebCT*. Britain and Liber conducted a survey among UK Higher Education institutions to ascertain the level of usage of VLEs and discovered that out of eleven respondents, nine institutions used them.[8] In these VLEs, the Web plays a pivotal role, around which all other aspects of the course of study evolve: students can type up an essay or assignment on word processor and send it by attachment on e-mail to their tutors, for example. They can also access CAL packages on-line. The Open University teaches many courses on-line, using VLEs. The *Lexica On-line* course for language learning is a good example. This Web-based package develops lexical skills and encourages students to use the target language (French) to communicate with one another (Goodfellow and Lamy 1998: 68).

The ability to use the Web for every aspect of a course of study is certainly advantageous for students on distance-learning courses, who are separated from the tutor and university facilities by large distances or other commitments such as job or a family that prevent those students from regularly attending a university campus. Nonetheless, many undergraduate courses are not distance-learning courses and

8   See Britain, S and Liber, O, 'A framework for pedagogical evaluation of virtual learning environments' as part of the Joint Information Systems Committee Technology Applications Programme at: http://www.jtap.ac.uk/reports/htm/jtap-041.html: due to low level of return, they were unable to perform a detailed analysis of the results.

students regularly attend campus. In that case, what purpose do VLEs serve? Surely, if students can access lecture notes, submit course assignments and keep in regular contact with their tutor using the Web, from the comfort of their own home, do they really need to attend the university for anything other than examinations or borrowing and returning library books, which also become obsolete with the advent of on-line and electronic publications?

Under UK Government proposals (the Dearing Report into Higher Education, for example), all students will be expected to have their own computer, probably a laptop or student personal computer (SPC) and will be connected to the Internet and other networked resources (Sosabowski, Herson and Lloyd 1998: 28). This could mean in theory that fewer students would physically attend university because they could fulfil most of the course requirements across the Web, which, in turn, would have consequences for the maintenance of university facilities, such as large lecture theatres and classrooms. In addition, the potential lack of physical contact between students and tutors that may result from using VLEs in this way will have a pernicious effect on one of the key aspects of university life: social interaction and personal development, enjoyment and entertainment. This was discussed during a debate on e-universities at the ALT Conference in Manchester (September 2000). During the debate, many speakers voiced their opinion that students attend university, not just for academic reasons, but also to satisfy the common human need for social contact and personal development; it is very difficult to satisfy these needs in a virtual environment. Not surprisingly, the motion of the debate ('without the e-university, HE in the UK is dead') was overwhelmingly defeated: a fitting demonstration of the importance that many academics attach to the traditional university environment. Designing a learning environment entirely around computer technology is often not appropriate in most university contexts, where traditional staff-student contact and interaction is essential. In addition, the creation of an exclusively computer-based environment is often impractical.[9] At the same time, however, technology offers potentially synergetic qualities.

Some university courses have introduced VLEs as an enhancement, instead of a replacement to conventional classes. The model adopted by the Italian Department at the University of Coventry is an example. There, students of Italian use *WebCT* to access administrative announcements, timetables and other notices about class arrangements, links to language resources and exercises that are dispersed across the Web. Tutors can send messages to individual students. The site also allows students to take part in on-line seminar discussions (Orsini-Jones 1999: 70). On-line discussions do not take place in real time, thereby allowing students and tutors to participate and contribute ideas when convenient. It also means that class time can be used for other activities, possibly oral work. The Coventry example shows that in a course based on campus, the Web can be a used alongside traditional classes, providing students with access to a wide range of material and information, in addition to facilitating communication, through on-line discussions and mail tools.

User requirements of a computer-based language-learning environment

Creating a computer-based environment involves the integration of computer technology into the four main elements of the environment. This, however, does not necessarily guarantee the effectiveness of the environment. In order to be successful, the environment needs to meet the needs of learners and teachers. Whereas the ultimate goal of any learning environment is its pedagogical effectiveness, there are a

9   During her keynote address at the 2000 ALT conference, Laurillard described that the use of ICT in 40% of learning activities would mean an increase of 50% in the input time required by academic staff and a 120% increase in the time required by production and technical staff.

number of other requirements or expectations of a computer-based model.

Technical requirements – reliability and access

It was once said that 'to err is human but to really foul things up requires a computer.'[10] The computer is sometimes not always the panacea that it is thought to be. Just like videos, overhead projectors and language laboratory equipment, computers suffer mechanical breakdown on occasions. Furthermore, when they fail to function, this can cause another problem: psychological demotivation. (Esch and Zähner, 2000: 12). If students are expected to use computers with regularity, it is not unreasonable to hope that ICT facilities will not be so unreliable that they become a barrier in students' work, rather than an aid. At present, many students use communal computing laboratories. The machines in these labs are subjected to immense pressure. Gillespie and McKee (1999a: 40) explain that in their experience, students can find weaknesses in CALL programs that software designers and programmers never dreamt possible. This is not exclusive to CALL programs: students can unwittingly add or delete files that cause conflicts in the system software: some do not know how to turn off (or even turn on) a computer properly, while others propagate viruses. They can do so in spite of the best efforts of computer technicians and computer centre staff to protect both the hardware and software and prevent unauthorised deleting of system files or applications. At the same time, however, students may require a certain degree of freedom to download applications from the WWW or other networked resource: this would not be possible if all software and hardware is write-protected. Moreover, language learners may wish to access target language television or radio channels across the Web for some aural practice: they may be unable to do so in certain labs because the necessary applications, like Windows Media Player and RealAudio Player cannot be downloaded or accessed and possibly

10   Quotation from 'Farmers' Almanac for 1978: Capsules of Wisdom'

even the necessary graphics or sound cards are not installed in the machines. The equipment needs regular monitoring and upgrading to ensure optimal performance, otherwise there is a great danger that students will vote with their feet and choose not to use equipment that they perceive to be antiquated and unreliable. If students feel discouraged about using ICT technology because of technical reliability or hardware/software limitations, it will be very difficult to encourage them to use a computer-based learning environment. Oliva and Pollastrini's (1995: 556) experience at the University of Utah is a good illustration of this. There efforts to develop a computer-based language-learning environment in the Department of Italian were hampered by technical problems, causing frustration among users.

Likewise, reliable hardware and software is dependant on connection to reliable, fast and flexible networks. In an environment for language learning, students will use CALL programs. Students may wish to use CALL packages in their own time, rather than in relation to class activities. An increasing number of institutions provide CALL laboratories where students can access networked CALL programs. They may, however, be unable to use the CALL lab and prefer to access CALL from another computing facility, possibly even at home or in a student residence, which might not give access to the CALL network. In the same way, institutions use multiple local area networks; certain computing labs may have access to some networks and not to others and some networks can be platform-dependent. Similarly, students may not have e-mail access in all labs because of networking considerations. This could be particularly problematic for students who take modules in different faculties: modern languages degrees are good examples. Here, students might have the option of taking modules that are not related to languages: business, law, informatics and even science. These students may need to use one network for their language modules and another to access information or resources for their non-language subjects.

One way of ensuring technical reliability would be to equip all students with their own personal computer (probably a laptop), which, would ensure that all students have access to similar specification computers, running state-of-the-art software. The provision of such a bank of computers would be cost prohibitive if the costs were borne by institutions, although possible sources of funding may be sought in industry or in hardware and software companies. Furthermore, institutions would be able to make certain savings by reducing the number of corporate general-purpose computer laboratories, providing print terminals and network portals instead.

It is equally important that, as far as possible, the social needs of staff and students can be accommodated within the learning environment. In her keynote address at the 2000 ALT conference, Diana Laurillard explained that, increasingly, students take on part-time jobs whilst at university to fund their studies, leading to demand for reduced class contact, and she argued that this needs to be taken into consideration in a learning environment. In addition, student work patterns are varied: those who have part-time jobs may find themselves working on essays or other assignments late in the evening or very early in the morning. Others, who have less class contact hours, may find themselves working at more regular times. CALL programs are a useful way of reducing class contact time in modern languages degrees, in the area of grammar for example, enabling more meaningful or possibly reduced class contact time. Equally, the Internet is very beneficial for sending or receiving work or messages at strange times. In other words, computer technology has the potential to facilitate more flexible learning patterns, although students need suitable access to resources and equipment. If students are working from home or from a university residence, such factors as adequate access to university network facilities, like e-mail accounts or computer conferencing systems, in addition to adequate hardware and software to type up essays and other work are important. A lack of satisfactory Internet access in the homes of students enrolled on a part-time campus-based MBA course at the University of Glasgow was one of the reasons for reduced participation in a CMC project (Boddy 1999: 43). If these facilities are not available in residence or term-time accommodation, students require adequate access (maybe 24-hour access) to computing labs in the university so that they can use them at times that they find convenient. In their report on Communications and Information Technology, Ron Dearing and his committee recommended that a ratio of eight students to one desktop computer is needed in UK universities if students are expected to make extensive use of on-line learning materials and information services, although a ratio of 5:1 would be desirable.[11] If access to computer facilities is very limited, this could justifiably drive students back to the apparent safety and comfort of pen and paper.

Psychological requirements – technical support and training

When technical problems occur, students and staff need suitable guidance and help. It is impractical to expect students and all teaching staff to know what to do if a computer crashes, a disk contracts a virus or a printing problem occurs, although as Gillespie and McKee (1999a: 40) discovered, students who have some knowledge about computers are more likely to attempt to solve computing problems themselves than students with basic computing skills. For many students, however, when technical difficulties occur, they are unable to deal with them and need help. Help-line links to computer services staff or technicians are important. Some staff who want to incorporate the computer into their teaching may not have the time, interest or ability to deal with the technical intricacies of developing CALL software etc and will prefer to entrust that to staff with adequate technical knowledge, allowing the academic staff to concentrate on the end result – using the software or other facilities in their classes. Such personnel may take the form of CALL development officers or technicians in CALL computing labs. These people could also provide technical support for students. Alternatively, the availability of postgraduate students near the computer facilities may provide students with an effective help-line because they may find it easier to talk to postgraduates and feel less inhibited about bringing problems to them.

Another way of providing adequate technical support is to provide suitable induction, explaining how programs work, encouraging

---

11 'National Report –Communications and Information Technology' in *The Dearing Report into Higher Education: Higher Education in the Learning Society*, HMSO 1997, Section 13.51. Accessed on WWW, August 2002 –http://www. leeds.ac.uk/educol/ncihe/nr_211.htm

good disk management and practice and explaining what to do when things go wrong. It is, of course, difficult to provide every student with an adequate level of technical induction that will enable them to deal with many of the problems they are likely to experience when using a computer: some students will demonstrate more willingness to learn how to deal with problems; for others, this is too complicated. Gillespie and McKee (1999a: 42) discovered that students are more nervous working with the computer than with pen and paper. They conclude that adequate induction is required so that students do not feel isolated when working with computers. If students feel that they are capable of dealing with most of the problems that they may face when using the computer, it stands to reason that they ought to feel less intimidated by the machine. This is one more step towards removing the psychological barriers associated with using computers and towards making the technology an invisible but significant part of the learning environment. Induction can take various forms, from paper-based manuals to interactive workshops but the purpose of them is to ensure that students feel more comfortable with the technology.

Induction is not exclusive to students: academic staff also require appropriate training, not least because students are likely to bring problems to them before approaching a technician or engineer. If students feel that academic staff are technologically illiterate, there is a danger that this will discourage them from using computers, with the attitude: 'if they do not understand or use computers, why should we?' A competent grounding in computer skills and a grasp of how to deal with problems will not always be enough to deal with every difficulty that students and staff face when using the computer but it will enable them to deal with the more basic problems; for the more serious problems like machine or network failure, expert help will still be necessary.

Obviously, university life extends beyond the classroom and the learning environment will need to reflect this. A language-learning environment will not just be limited to a CALL or faculty computer lab, a series of language laboratories or networked SPCs. Students will require access to other resources like library facilities to reserve books or renew loans; the examinations office to obtain timetabling information or results and computer services for the type of technical support outlined above. Martin (1997: 6) advocates this idea and suggests that integration of facilities is necessary to ensure that staff and students have access to a seamless web of information and material. In addition, they might wish to access material or resources at other institutions, language centres for example. Unlike most other courses, languages students may need to contact staff or students in target language universities, in an effort to gather information about that institution in preparation for their residence abroad. The more access students have to a wide range of facilities, the more comfortable they ought to feel with the computer and the more confidence they could have in using the computer in the learning process: such an opinion is reflected by Gillespie and McKee (1999a: 43). In their survey on student opinion towards the Internet, they discovered that students found the Internet useful because a plethora of information could be accessed from one computer terminal and they did not need to move from place to place to gather material.

One way of bringing many university facilities and resources closer to the student through computer technology could be to adopt a single desktop environment. In such an environment, each student has password-protected access to his own exclusive desktop and server space. Students can save files in their personal server space in total security. Their desktop is customised to provide them with specific applications that they may require, like CALL programs, CMC or e-mail systems and library catalogues.

Wenger (1996: 58) argues that institutional support is required to secure funding needed in order to install the computer equipment necessary to make a computer-based environment workable. In addition, King *et al.* (1998: 15) and Kassen and Higgins (1997: 264) both highlight the importance of support at the highest level is important to encourage departmental staff to make the leap into technology and to feel that their work will be regarded with importance and not viewed as a personal hobby. Staff involved in computer-based learning spend many hours transferring material like lecture notes to the computer, preparing websites and developing CALL programs. Unsympathetic senior managers may only allow staff to work on these projects in their own time and not consider the creation of electronic courseware as worthwhile activities, both in terms of pedagogical and research development. This would certainly have serious implications for computer-based learning projects and may hamper efforts to create a computer-based environment.

Although institutional support is fundamental, without the support of teaching colleagues, efforts to design a computer-based environment seem fruitless. Since departmental colleagues will be expected to implement and use the environment, it would seem pointless to create an environment that was only used by one or two members of staff and rejected by the rest. It would be equally frustrating and confusing for students because some staff would use it regularly to send notes and other information and encourage students to use the computer prodigiously to send or receive work, whilst others would oppose such technological methods of course delivery. Nevertheless, it can be very difficult to encourage members of staff who are so entrenched in their own traditional methods of course delivery that they resist any suggestion of change. Likewise there are those who are fearful or unwilling to embrace a new technology-based environment (Gillespie and Barr, 2002: 120–32). If a computer-based learning environment is going to work and be used effectively, it needs to be universally adopted by staff. Computer-based projects can founder or experience great difficulty unless staff involved are equally committed: the lessons learned by Gillespie and Barr in the Châteauroux project are an interesting illustration of this.[12]

12   Gillespie and Barr, 'Châteauroux project: a pilot study in the use of *FirstClass* for tandem learning'. Paper delivered at EUROCALL 2000, September 2000, University of Abertay, Dundee Scotland

If staff are to embrace the technology, they need to feel that it is beneficial. Zakrzewski and Bull (1997: 6) discovered that staff reacted negatively to *Transmath*, a mathematical CAL package tested at the University of Luton, because it did not reduce contact time with students and required staff to spend considerable time helping and guiding students in the use of the package. Reduction in staff-student contact time or, at least, the notion that it can lead to more meaningful and productive contact hours is one of the great boasts of CALL and it is hardly surprising that the prospect of spending considerable periods of time teaching students how to use programs or resolving problems that arise from hardware and software failure can lead staff to consider the computer as more of a hindrance than a help in the classroom. Kassen and Higgins (1997: 265) believe that one way of showing colleagues the benefit of learning technology is to ensure sustained training sessions for staff in the use of computers in language teaching. Examples of this type of training include the Catholic University of America, which arranges workshops to train staff, and the ICT4LT (Information and Communication Technology for Language Teachers) on-line modular course, available to secondary and tertiary-level language teachers, mainly in Europe.[13]

For staff who are reluctant to embrace the technological challenge, it may be necessary to impose and enforce environment implementation from above: such an approach is recommended by the Joint Information Systems Committee (JISC) in their report on Managed Learning Environments.[14] A top-down approach can, of course, have the adverse effect of causing friction and animosity among some staff, and may even discourage those proponents of the computer-based environment who feel that their idea is being poached by others, although it could be a necessary evil: if staff are not kick-started into implementing and using an environment, it may never

---

13 See Kassen and Higgins (1997: 269) and ICT4LT website, accessed May 2002: http://www.ict4lt.org
14 See JISC (Joint Information Systems Committee) workshop final report on Managed Learning Environments, Retrieved from the WWW: http://www.jisc. ac.uk/pub00/mle/final_rep.html: January 2001

become fully operational and staff involved, as well as students, may lose motivation and feel the environment will not work.

Examples of computer-based language-learning environments: choice of case studies and methodology

In order to evaluate how effectively computer technology has been endorsed in the language learning and teaching environment, three higher education establishments have been chosen for examination. These are the Universities of Ulster, Cambridge and Toronto. The choice of a high profile and historical institution (Cambridge), alongside a newer university (Ulster) demonstrates the wide diversity of reaction to computer-based learning and provision of electronic language learning facilities that currently exists, not just in Britain, but also potentially across Europe. Toronto, long internationally recognised as one of the world leaders in the use of computer technology in learning and teaching, was chosen as an international benchmark. Each case study will reveal examples of innovative practice and areas for improvement will be identified. Furthermore, the choice of case studies is designed to show the extent to which the use of technology is dependant on the character of each institution.

A number of methods have been used to analyse the centrality of computer technology in the language-learning environment of each institution. These include extensive observational analysis during three-week research visits to Cambridge and Toronto between February and April 2001. Follow-up analysis was carried out through e-mail contact with members of staff in each university and through consultation with the regularly updated departmental and institutional websites. At Ulster, the home institution for this study, observational analysis was conducted over a period of three years. Secondly, students and staff from a range of languages departments were asked to complete separate questionnaires. A total of sixty-eight staff and two hundred and eighteen student questionnaires were returned. In addition to these methods of data collection, information was also obtained through interviews with key members of academic and technical staff in all three universities and through focus groups with cohorts of students from different years and language disciplines.

Chapter Three
Example 1: the University of Ulster

Background information

The University of Ulster is the youngest of the three institutions studied.

History

Established in 1984 as a result of a merger between the New University of Ulster and the Ulster Polytechnic, the University of Ulster (UU) is the largest third level educational establishment in Ireland. Today there are approximately twenty-two thousand full-time and part-time students on four campuses spread across Northern Ireland: Coleraine (the administrative headquarters), Jordanstown (on the outskirts of Belfast), Magee (in Londonderry) and Belfast. Although the University is centrally managed and staff teach across campuses, each campus has its own student base and offers courses specific to that campus. In addition to providing many full-time degree courses, the University offers a large number of part-time diplomas and degrees and is developing e-learning courses for mature students: at present, it has more mature students than any other UK institution, apart from the Open University.

Students tend to live on or near their campus during term-time: the University provides accommodation for a total of approximately 2100 students, most of whom are first year students, postgraduates or international students, housing them in either traditional halls of residence or in University-leased accommodation blocks off-campus. This is a small proportion of the entire UU student population. Most others live in private accommodation in the cities of Belfast or Londonderry and the smaller seaside towns of Portrush and Portstewart, which are located approximately four miles from the Coleraine campus. Furthermore, some students commute each day from home, usually to reduce expense or because of family or employment commitments. Students, therefore, are dispersed over a wide area during term time: some may live a few hundred metres from campus while others live fifty or sixty miles away.

Modern languages at Ulster

Language teaching at Ulster is the responsibility of the School of Languages and Literature (in the Faculty of Arts), which is divided into eight subjects: American Studies, English, European Studies, Irish, French, German, Japanese and Spanish and a total of eighty full and part-time academic staff teach these subjects on the four campuses. Each subject has its own head and they liase with the Head of School. The bulk of the language teaching takes place on two campuses – Coleraine and Magee, where six main language courses are provided: Humanities Combined (which offers a range of subjects, from literature to area studies), Applied Languages, Irish Studies, International Business Communication, International Business Studies and the postgraduate diploma/MA in Applied Languages for Business. Of the four current undergraduate courses, one is a specialist language course – Applied Languages, where students specialise in two languages to degree level (a choice from French, German and Spanish). The Jordanstown campus provides a postgraduate diploma and Masters degree in Modern French Studies: most of the students taking this course are secondary school French teachers. The campuses provides a number of non-specialist language options in Modern Languages on undergraduate courses in other faculties, Engineering, for example. At present, there are over five hundred students taking specialist language courses and three to four hundred enrolled in non-specialist options. Teaching, though, is generally conducted in small groups.

Most members of staff in Modern Languages are based on the Coleraine and Magee campuses and a number of them teach courses on both campuses. Languages staff have permanent offices on the campus where they carry out the bulk of their teaching. On the Coleraine and Magee sites, all language staff offices are usually situated in the same building. On both campuses, language students have a communal area – the *médiathèque*. They use this area for private study, watching satellite broadcasts, for example, or work with classmates to prepare presentations or other joint projects: students who commute from home each day sometimes use the médiathèque as their base and work from there when they are not in class. The facility is equipped with a range of language reference material such as dictionaries, grammar books and area studies notes: on the Coleraine campus, this centre is located beside a small computer lab. Staff offices, including the School secretaries' offices, are located nearby, along with course and subject noticeboards and seminar teaching rooms. Students have classes every day on the Coleraine and Magee sites and even if these take place on the other side of campus, students are never more than five to ten minutes walk from the médiathèque and other facilities such as course noticeboards, which students consult regularly. Consequently, the two buildings mentioned above are focal points for languages staff and students at Ulster. At Jordanstown, such a focal point does not exist, due in no small part to the fact that there are very few languages staff based on this campus and that the main languages degree offered at Jordanstown is a postgraduate part-time course where students have three hours of classes per week. The presence of languages staff, students and facilities is therefore less noticeable on that site than at Magee and Coleraine and, as a result, most of the observations made here refer in particular to language learning on those two campuses.

Computer infrastructure

It has already been established that an efficient infrastructure is required to ensure that the computer can be used to maximal effect in a language-learning environment. A number of observations can be made about the Ulster infrastructure.

Computer provision/management

Despite being dispersed across four campuses, the University of Ulster is a highly centralised institution, from senior management level to library and computing facilities. The computer facilities are managed and provided at two levels.

Firstly, IT User Services (who are based on each campus with their main office at Jordanstown) control and maintain over sixty student corporate computer labs on all campuses, providing access to over one thousand five hundred workstations. In addition, IT User Services maintains most of the mail servers for staff and students (the Faculty of Informatics maintain their own) and manages the University's network backbone. Although some labs have newer hardware than others, IT User Services provide a standard range of software in all student corporate labs through a Common Desktop Environment or CDE, allowing them to upgrade and change software across all labs with relative ease. In October 2001, all corporate labs began operating a personal login feature, using Novell networking, known as the single sign-on facility (SSO). This provides students with 25 MB of their own secure server space to save documents and store e-mails, accessible from corporate labs on any campus. IT User Services intends to operate a Web portal to allow students to access files and messages stored on their SSO account and to transfer files to and from an external PC, either at home or in residence, for example. The SSO facility is currently only available to undergraduate students, although if successful, it is hoped to make it available to staff also. Although there are a number of general use corporate labs, there is usually at least one located in each faculty building and IT User Services provide a number of faculty or subject-specific applications in those labs. The labs are used for teaching and private study and they are heavily booked for teaching purposes during term-time, with preference generally given to staff from the local faculty. Although many corporate computer labs are faculty-orientated, there are a small proportion of labs that are controlled locally by a faculty or school. One of these is currently located in the Faculty of Arts' médiathèque on the Coleraine campus, which operates a Mac platform, works outside the Common Desktop Environment and is not managed or funded by IT User Services. This type of faculty-run lab is gradually disappearing and within a few years, most of the labs will be centrally run and operate a PC platform.

Secondly, although the provision of corporate computer labs means that very few faculties need to manage their own labs, they, rather than IT User Services, are responsible for the provision of staff computing facilities. Each faculty appoints its own technicians who are responsible for and maintaining staff computers and for purchasing hardware and software on behalf on the schools.

Networking infrastructure

Networking provision and Internet access is generally uniform across the University. Every teaching room and office is connected to Ulster's network backbone. The network was upgraded at the start of the 2001/02 academic year, enabling it to deal with more network traffic and simultaneous users. Network access is partially available in University accommodation on campus. There are no immediate plans to provide network access to the University-leased houses and flats off-campus. The vast majority of students do not live in any form of University accommodation and network and Internet access for these students is more problematic. Furthermore, few students who live in rented accommodation have access to telephone lines – landlords tend not to be prepared to give students access to telephone lines from their own bedrooms, but rather install communal payphones to avoid problems of non-payment of telephone bills. Whereas an increasing numbers of students commute to University each day from the parental home, where they have Internet access, it is difficult to imagine that Internet and network access will become available to majority of students off campus in their term-time accommodation.

E-mail provision

Since the University of Ulster is spread across Northern Ireland, fast and efficient communication is essential. The University operates an internal mail service, however it may take a few days for correspondence to be delivered to another campus, forty or fifty miles away. E-mail is a quicker means of communication and has become well established throughout the University. The University provides an ever-improving e-mail infrastructure. Operating a gamut of mail servers that are based on each campus, over three thousand members of staff and all students are provided with e-mail accounts by IT User Services.

All students are automatically issued with e-mail accounts as soon as they join the University. Under the current arrangements, all incoming students are registered for e-mail and allocated an e-mail address when they accept a place at the University. They are then given an information pack at official registration. This pack contains a PIN code, which students use to activate their e-mail accounts using a basic electronic authentication procedure that can only be accessed from computers on campus. The e-mail addresses of all students, whether or not they have activated their accounts, are published by the Academic Registry on the on-line module and course database, usually within a few days of official student registration at the beginning of the academic year. This allows interested staff to create their own e-mail distribution lists for courses or modules they teach.

E-mail access has generally been restricted with some exceptions, to use on campus and staff who are teaching on a different campus (for example staff based in Magee but who are teaching in Coleraine one or two days per week) cannot access their e-mail accounts in the corporate computer labs or Library computing facilities on that campus. In other words, staff and students cannot access their University e-mail whenever and wherever they want. Whereas e-mail is obviously a useful means of staff-student communication, especially across campuses based in different towns and cities, the limitations of the Ulster system make it a less effective means of communication than it could be. This problem is being largely addressed by the ongoing implementation of a webmail service for staff and students.

Computer-based language learning in action

The computer is used for language learning and teaching purposes at Ulster in two main ways: to facilitate staff-student communication and to provide a range of electronic resources and language learning and teaching material and resources. Information on the use of computer technology has been drawn from the findings of student and staff questionnaires, interviews and observational reports from students in first, second and final years on the Magee and Coleraine campuses. Questionnaires were administered on paper to students and through e-mail and hard copy to staff. In addition, questionnaires that formed part of a separate research project, mapping the use of *FirstClass*, have also been used in this analysis. Seventy-two completed surveys were received from students and thirteen from staff on both campuses.

Computer-mediated communication:
e-mail versus computer conferencing

Even though noticeboards have traditionally been used to convey information to students, staff have moved towards electronic com-munication. They recognise that it is a more effective way of sending information to students, especially for those students who commute to university from home or are studying on part-time courses (the Diplo-ma/MA in Modern French Studies, for example). The value of elec-tronic communication is clear, too, for staff who teach students on other campuses. E-mail appears the most obvious choice for electronic communication since all staff and students are now automatically is-sued with accounts. In the School of Languages and Literature, how-ever, e-mail has not been adopted as the principal means of communication. Networking problems in the Faculty computer room and in the languages computer room in the médiathèque on the Coleraine campus meant that students could not access their University e-mail accounts. In 1996, the School sought to address this problem and implement a common communications package that would be used by staff and students alike. That year, it introduced *FirstClass*, the computer conferencing package from *Softarc*, to its staff and students and this package has now been adopted on three campuses. It is now used by staff and students in other faculties and schools, especially the School of Nursing and the School of Biomedical Sciences. At present, there are over 700 licensed users in the University.

Within the School of Languages and Literature, staff in French, German and Spanish use *FirstClass* to send coursework information, such as essay titles, lecture notes, administrative information relating to modules or courses and coursework marks to students. The enhanced functionality of *FirstClass* makes it easy for staff and students to send and receive attachments, and students – especially in French and Spanish – use this feature to submit essays, translations and other forms of coursework. *FirstClass* has proved useful to overcome problems of platform incompatibility. Until recently, most members of staff in the School used Macintosh computers, running a highly restrictive e-mail client, while many students would use the corporate PC labs to access their e-mail. Consequently, it was very difficult to receive and open attachments sent from another Macintosh computer, not to mention the problems experienced when endeavouring to open an attachment sent from a PC. With *FirstClass*, work can be sent from a PC and opened on a Mac and vice versa, providing acceptable file formats are used. This is supported by the results from the 1999 *FirstClass* questionnaire, which discovered that 83% of staff respondents (N=6) considered it to be a better means of communication than e-mail. Since the beginning of the 2001/02 academic year, the majority of staff in Modern Languages, with one or two exceptions, are now using PCs and versions of software that are compatible with student PCs (according to the findings of a follow-up questionnaire administered to Ulster staff in 2001/02, 82%, where N=11, were using a PC, compared to 62%, where N=13, in 2000/01). This means that staff and students can now use the University e-mail system to send and receive attachments, such as essays or other coursework, in addition to using *FirstClass* for this purpose.

Until recently, *FirstClass* was only available as a client user package on internal University computers. Since the beginning of the 1999/2000 academic year, users have been able to access their accounts across the Web, following the creation of a browser interface for *FirstClass*. This addition has enhanced the way that *FirstClass* is used, allowing staff and students to consult their accounts and send and receive work from anywhere in the world, at any time. This has proved especially useful for students on their year abroad in France, Spain, Belgium and Germany who can maintain regular contact with staff back at the UU and send dissertation chapter drafts or plans to their supervisors. Likewise, students enrolled on part-time courses and those who live at home can maintain regular contact with staff and stay informed about course or module developments without attending campus every day.

IT User Services on the Coleraine campus are responsible for maintaining *FirstClass*, providing a server and taking charge of the general administration of the system. In addition, three co-ordinators have been appointed among teaching staff in the School of Languages and Literature, charged with the daily, non-technical maintenance of the conferencing system. On the Coleraine campus, each language module has been assigned a conference and the co-ordinators ensure that all students enrolled in each module, as well as teaching staff responsible for delivery of classes, have access to appropriate conferences. This means that when staff send messages to the conference that corresponds to the module they teach, all students in that module receive the message. On the Magee campus, a less elaborate system is used, with conferences corresponding to subject and year groups rather than module codes.

Some members of staff have used *FirstClass* as an alternative to Web publishing. Material published on *FirstClass* is restricted by password and username and this allows staff to publish material that they may wish to restrict to students or colleagues on a particular course or module only. This has allowed members of staff involved in preparation of students for their year abroad to publish notes about destinations and guidelines about living in the target language countries on-line, allowing those students to access this material when they are abroad. User guides, explaining how to use computer programs like MS Word, PowerPoint, and *FirstClass* – material that may not be freely available to everyone on the Web because of copyright or other implications have been made available on-line using this conferencing program.

The academic year 2000/01 saw the introduction of an electronic noticeboard or 'Bulletin Board' for languages staff and students on the Coleraine campus. Staff and students alike use this conference to publish material or pass on information that is of general interest and is not exclusive to particular modules. Examination and semester timetables, along with details of social events, minutes and details of meetings and advice to students are among some of the information that is published on the Bulletin Board.

The extensive use of *FirstClass* does not mean that e-mail has become redundant as a means of communication. E-mail is used for the vast bulk of administrative communication because staff tend to consult their e-mail more regularly than their *FirstClass* accounts and official memos and other information from the Faculty of Arts and administrative departments in the University are circulated by e-mail. Furthermore, in recent years, the *FirstClass* system has been plagued with technical difficulties, mainly due to an explosion in traffic using the *FirstClass* server. Whereas most of these difficulties have been resolved with the installation of a new, faster server, the conferencing system is still not as reliable as it ought to be with the Web browser interface of *FirstClass* crashing at least once a week because of server software conflicts that have yet to be resolved. This problem has led to students and staff being unable to access their accounts on *FirstClass* at certain times, preventing them from accessing information or sending and receiving messages on those occasions. The e-mail servers tend to be very reliable, with few server outages, except for essential maintenance work.

Although e-mail and *FirstClass* are largely used for communication, over the past few years languages staff have used them in language learning projects. In 1999/2000, two colleagues from French established a tandem learning project between first year Applied Languages students of French at Ulster and a group of Business Studies students from the University of Orléans in France, with all communication between students taking place via *FirstClass*. The Ulster students had to complete a translation exercise and send it to their partners in France, who were then expected to make corrections and return the amended scripts electronically. One of the positive outcomes of the tandem experiment was that *FirstClass* proved to be a useful way of monitoring students' progress at each stage of the project since all messages and work were stored on one server and could be easily accessed by the project co-ordinators. Three years earlier, a colleague from Spanish set up a similar project between the Universities of Ulster and Vigo, in Spain. That project used e-mail as the means of communication and this proved to be its failing, partly due to the networking problems at Ulster, which meant that students could not use e-mail in the Faculty computing labs that were Mac based (where they would type up most of their work) and instead had to use PC facilities, which caused several compatibility problems.

Although *FirstClass* and e-mail are used by both staff and students, questionnaire findings indicate that the former is the preferred method of communication. There is also a disparity in the way that staff and students communicate electronically.

Questionnaire evidence shows that languages staff use e-mail quite extensively. 92% of respondents (unless otherwise stated, N=13) confirmed they use e-mail regularly for University work. Staff confirmed that their main reason for using it is to communicate with colleagues (85%), while a much reduced proportion (54%) use it to communicate with students. 23% and 31% of colleagues use e-mail to receive and send work to students respectively. This tends to suggest that e-mail is used for course administration matters and is not used in mainstream language teaching. One reason for this trend may be the difficulties associated with the e-mail client on earlier versions of

Macintosh computers, which made it difficult sending and receiving attachments. In other words, staff have really only used that e-mail system to send simple, unformatted messages – and not to send work in attachment form or text with complex formatting. Similarly, students have tended not to send work to staff by e-mail because of the difficulty opening it as an attachment. Despite the arrival of new PCs for staff, with an improved e-mail interface for attachments, it would seem that is has not encouraged more staff to use e-mail for sending and receiving work. According to the results of the follow-up staff questionnaire administered in April 2002 after the installation of new PC hardware (see Appendix 1c), 27% of colleagues used e-mail regularly to send and receive coursework to and from their students (N=11). This compares to the results of the initial questionnaire that was administered before the arrival of new hardware, which revealed that 23% used it frequently to receive coursework and 31% who sent work to students (N=13). These results suggest that hardware and software do not seem to crucial factors in encouraging staff to send and receive work electronically. They imply, however, that a more important factor is the development of an e-culture to make the electronic transmission of work a very natural part of the learning environment. In other words, if staff (and students) become so familiar with the concept of electronic transmission of work or other documentation, it will become just as natural to them as using the conventional methods. Furthermore, the development of an impetus to communicate electronically also serves to encourage others who may be less willing to embrace this technology because of necessity or desire not to be left behind.

Staff are more willing to use *FirstClass* as part of their mainstream teaching. In 1999, 90% (N=10) used it to send lecture notes to students and 60% received coursework from students through the system, normally as attachments. All respondents in that survey said they used *FirstClass* to contact their classes. In addition, half of the respondents admitted using it to return marked work. This implies that around half of the staff have either corrected work on-screen or have simply sent comments and evaluative feedback to students about their work electronically. The degree to which staff use electronic communication for receiving or correcting coursework varies across the cohort of staff: some are obviously very comfortable with its use, while others feel it is too time consuming, costly (i.e. printing out student work in order to mark it) or very difficult (marking work on-screen). Since a significant proportion of staff is prepared to embrace it, this demonstrates a willingness to use electronic communication in the process of administering coursework, thereby also encouraging students to embrace the technology, by using it to submit work. There are a number of reasons that explain why *FirstClass* is used in the teaching process more than e-mail. Firstly, staff may prefer to keep messages relating to coursework and administration separate from those relating to teaching. By using the two systems, staff can avoid clogging up their e-mail accounts with student coursework, which they can store on *FirstClass*. It is also easier to send messages to groups of students, enrolled in particular modules, for example, on *FirstClass* instead of e-mail. If staff want to send e-mail messages to students enrolled in a particular module, they have to create their own distribution lists – none are provided by Academic Registry or the Faculty of Arts. Although this is not a complex procedure, it can be time consuming. Whereas, although it is equally time-consuming add-ing students to conferences on *FirstClass*, one member of staff norm-ally undertakes this for all languages staff, meaning that colleagues do not have to concern themselves with such technical intricacies. These intricacies can prove very daunting for some staff who are interested in the end result – using it to communicate with students – but do not want the burden of setting up the technology. The success of *First-Class* suggests that if the technology is invisible and does not require a great deal of effort by staff to set it up, staff will use it more readily.

Personal use of e-mail among students is higher than among staff (85% of students, where N=72, use e-mail this way in comparison to 62% of staff). Nevertheless, a reduced percentage of students use e-mail for academic purposes. 47% of respondents admitted using e-mail regularly for University-related tasks, its most common usage being as a means of communicating with friends at other universities (81% use e-mail for this purpose). 36% communicate with staff using e-mail. 21% and 38% respectively use e-mail to send and receive coursework from staff, confirming evidence taken from questionnaires administered to staff that shows that e-mail is not used widely as part of the learning and teaching experience in languages. This may be explained by poor Internet access in term-time accommodation (6% of students, where N=72, have term-time access). In order words, students do not have the flexibility to use the Internet at times most convenient for them, such as late in the evening when they are most likely to be preparing assignments and other coursework.

If this were the main reason to explain poor use of e-mail for academic purposes, the use of *FirstClass* would be equally poor. On the other hand, however, student usage of *FirstClass* is high. 84% (N=43) admitted in 1999 to using *FirstClass* for receiving and submitting coursework. This high figure is undoubtedly due in part to the endorsement by a substantial number of staff of this form of electronic communication to send and receive coursework. Although the findings of this research suggest that students tend to use e-mail more than staff outside the University context and therefore that there is more evidence of a general e-mail culture among students, clearly *FirstClass* is preferred for University communication. Although it was initially adopted, in part, to address the problem of poor e-mail facilities for languages students, the system is still heavily used, even though this problem is less acute. One reason for this is that all students (with a few exceptions in one of the languages that uses it) are automatically registered for *FirstClass*, unlike e-mail where students are required to activate e-mail accounts themselves, with the inevitable result that, in the past, many did not do so. The advent of the single sign-on facility, which requires students to activate their e-mail accounts if they want to log onto University PCs, means that the vast majority of students will now have active University e-mail accounts. Of course, this does not mean that the students will use their University e-mail. Many students already have Hotmail or other web-mail accounts and do not want the confusion of regularly checking multiple e-mail accounts. If students do not check their University e-mail accounts regularly, this makes it very difficult for staff to use it as a reliable means of communicating with students. If staff want to build a distribution list of e-mail accounts for modules, the most effective way to do so is to ask the students for their e-mail address for Hotmail in class. This, of course, is not fully reliable: staff have no way of checking whether students are using their accounts, unlike with the University e-mail system, which is fully logged. Furthermore, students use *FirstClass* extensively because they know that since staff rely on it to post up course material, if they do not check their *FirstClass* accounts regularly, then they are going to miss out on valuable information and notes. The high level of dependency on the use of *FirstClass*, which ensures its continued extensive use, is evidence of an e-culture among staff and students. This seems to have made it easier to integrate computer technology into the process of learning and teaching, therefore ensuring its centrality in the learning environment.

The success of *FirstClass* demonstrates that if students perceive pedagogical benefit from using technology, they will overcome problems such as poor access to it in term-time accommodation. They are prepared to take measures such as visiting a computer lab on campus late in the evening or calling in with a friend, who has Internet access, because they know they must use it to obtain notes, submit coursework or contact the tutor: it is not an optional extra.

Computer-mediated communication (CMC) is used extensively to facilitate staff-student contact and there is evidence of an electronic communications culture at this institution. The pattern of e-mail and *FirstClass* usage may change in the next few years because of the introduction of *Campus One* as the University's on-line learning environment, which will mean the eventual phasing out of *FirstClass*. The system, created on *WebCT*, is more advanced and complex than *FirstClass*, which, in turn, is marginally easier to use than e-mail. Although it is more functional than e-mail, staff may decide that e-mail is the simpler option. Furthermore, one reason for adopting *FirstClass* initially was to counteract the problem of networking incompatibility between student and staff computers, and these problems have largely disappeared.

Electronic resources: the World Wide Web

The University of Ulster operates a very strict policy on the use of its website. Effectively, since its Web pages are openly accessible throughout the world, all material that is published on the page is subject to fierce scrutiny and anything that may be considered detrimental to the image of the University will not be included on the website. The responsibility for scrutinising material and publishing it lies with a small body, known as the 'Online Group of Public Affairs' and faculty co-ordinating officers (although the role of these officers varies across faculties and some are more active in Web publishing than others). If members of staff wish to publish material on the University website, they are expected to contact the faculty co-ordinator, and then pass the material to Online Group who will publish the material. This is a lengthy process that can take several days, sometimes weeks. As a result, certain departments within the University, most notably the Library and the Faculty of Informatics operate their own Web servers, publishing material on an intranet that is normally openly accessible through the main University website. Although subject to the same standards and protocol as the material published by the Online Group, the Library and Faculty of Informatics can update and add material to their Web pages with greater rapidity, usually less than two days.

This restriction means that academic staff do not, generally, use the University website to publish course material and resources. With many other UK universities opening up the doors of Web publication to academic staff, the University of Ulster has recognised that it needs to catch up. A University taskforce, set up to examine the institution's ICT policy, recommended the creation of a series of intranets and extranets (external intranets) to enable staff to develop course materials and resources. Access to the extranets will be restricted by password and will be accessible from outside the University, although the material they provide will not be openly available on the main University website. *FirstClass* has, in effect, become one of the first extranets and only those who have accounts on *FirstClass* can access information published on it. One of the main drawbacks of this system, though, is that most of the material provided through *FirstClass*, whether lecture notes, coursework details or timetables, is created using word processing packages and sent as attachments. This may be suitable for text-based material but lacks the flexibility needed for sending audiovisual material – flexibility that is normally available when designing material using HTML editors and other Web-authoring software.

There is, though, some language-learning material openly available through the University's website. Library staff at Magee and Coleraine have published Web gateways containing useful external Web links, including on-line dictionaries and target language newspapers. On the Magee campus, these Web links have been prepared primarily for students on the International Business Communication degree programme. On the Coleraine campus, the gateway for French was revised in the 2000/01 academic year and one for Spanish created, offering links to self-correcting grammar exercises and notes, as well as political and other material that is useful for students taking area studies module options. The provision of these languages gateways is an obvious attempt to help students find language-learning material and resources on the Web with greater ease than spending countless hours sifting through copious results from search engines: a problem that Haworth (1996: 180) alludes to in his paper, 'The Internet as a language learning resource'.

During the 2001/02 academic year, languages colleagues decided to create a computer-based multiple-choice grammar diagnostics test as part of the yearly Language Audit. Using *Campus One*, tests were created for French, German and Spanish. First and final year students in Applied Languages and Humanities Combined were asked to complete the forty-question test paper in fifty minutes: each test was then automatically graded by *Campus One* and the results of each script, along with a break-down of student responses, were sent to tutors in each of the languages. This allowed staff to evaluate the linguistic level of each student and consider which areas of grammar were particularly deficient for most students. This, in turn, may allow staff to alter the grammar syllabus for each language in future years, to make it more relevant to the needs of the UU students. This supports the learning model suggested by Adamson (1998: 177), in which explicit grammar teaching (grammar theory classes) can be used to fill the gaps of implicit grammar (learning grammar through practice).

Given the difficulty that staff experience when trying to use the University website to publish material such as notes or to design Web-based exercises, only a small percentage of respondents to the staff questionnaire have used the Web for these purposes (23%, where N=13, have published notes on the Web, while none have designed on-line language-learning exercises). Most of them, however, use the Web regularly for teaching and learning purposes. 92% of staff respondents confirmed they browse the Web regularly for University-related tasks – the same percentage that frequently use e-mail. This obviously suggests that many of them consider the Web as an important part of their daily work. Tutors outlined two main uses of the Web: researching material for class and for academic research (62% of respondents confirmed they use it regularly for both activities). This further illustrates the importance of the Web for them because they can use it both for preparing class and as a means of pursuing research interests, indicating a high level of interaction with the Web. Its use as a source of reference for academic research reveals an interesting point: most academic staff are engaged in literature-based research and yet are obviously able to use the Web to find material that is of interest to their field of research. This appears to contradict the argument of some, including staff at the University, who argue that the Web is not a suitable or reliable place to search for material of a truly academic or literary nature. These staff also express concern that students will over-use the Web and neglect written books or articles. Nevertheless, many staff consider that the Web has a lot of accurate academic material that is obviously of immense value to students, otherwise they would not be willing to use it for their own research. This is an indirect endorsement of its utility.

Evidence of their belief in the value of the Web can be seen from the ways in which staff encourage their students to use the Web. 85% encourage them to use it to research material for coursework, while 77% invite students to use it for self-study, using it to access target language newspapers, on-line radio and television stations. One of the main reasons why both percentages are so high is that there is a lot of material on the Web that is suitable for the languages curriculum at Ulster. For example, many of the area studies topics covered in the French, Spanish and German, such as regionalism, contemporary politics, media and post-war German history, are well documented on the Web. In addition, the module outlines for Spanish courses on the Coleraine campus (in addition to French and Spanish courses at Magee) now contain comprehensive lists of websites in the bibliographies of recommended reading material. Some topics covered in area studies, for example, deal with events that have taken place so recently that they have not yet been published in books – the events of 11 September 2001 are a good example. In addition, the creation of Web gateways in some languages also provides students with a focal point when using the Web for research and therefore makes it more appealing to use it when preparing assignments.

One reason that may explain why staff feel it important to encourage students to use the Web to engage in self-study is the School of Language and Literature's approach to this issue. Students are regularly invited to use the médiathèques, created by the School on both the Magee and Coleraine campuses, to read target language newspapers or watch satellite television. Students are asked to spend at least one hour per week in the médiathèque for each language they study. The Web offers students access to such newspapers and television. Furthermore, it gives students the flexibility to use the material when they want or have the time to do so and therefore they are not dependent on the limited opening hours of the médiathèques. Aware of this, many staff have now begun to encourage students to use the Web for such activities in an effort to persuade them to engage in self-study more regularly.

Staff, however, seem to view the Web as a passive source of reference (similar to a library with both text-based and audiovisual media) and are not fully aware of its interactive potential. Questionnaire evidence supports that view: 8% of tutors encourage students to complete on-line language learning exercises. Perhaps the main reason for this lack of knowledge about the potential of the Web is a lack of training: this view is confirmed by another question in the survey, which found that 62% of staff felt they are not well trained and do not fully understand the potential that ICT offers them. This may also be the result of a teaching culture that is firmly rooted in a reference library culture, and many have seen the Web as a replacement for the old library system.

Results from the student questionnaire reflect those illustrated in the staff survey above. 81% of students regularly use the Web for University work. Two main uses of the Web were cited by students: 82% use it to research material for essays, while 65% use it to communicate with friends or members of staff, using webmail systems or synchronous chatrooms. 40% of students use the Web for self-study. This means that despite the best efforts of staff to exhort their students to use the Web for self-study purposes, many do not. On the other hand, however, many of the students will research material for essays and other forms of coursework, heeding the advice given by their tutors. There is one main reason for this: students know that they can use the Web to find a lot of material that is relevant to their areas of study and that by not doing so, they realise that they will miss out material that will help them to score better marks in coursework and examinations. Fewer choose to use the Web for self-study because, although it is beneficial to language learning, it is usually not directly assessed in any way and the students therefore give it less priority than work that is directly assessed. In principle, they may want to use Web-based material for self-study but in practice there may be little time for that luxury and their normal workload is enough of a struggle. This suggests that students are less likely to engage in self-study unless they receive some kind of academic credit for it, such as a coursework or participation mark. Like staff, few students seem aware of the interactive possibilities of the Web, with only 4% using on-line language learning exercises. Such a low percentage is hardly surprising given that few staff encourage students to use the Web interactively. This implies that students depend on members of staff to make them aware of the potential of the Web before they will use it – few of them have the necessary time (and self-motivation) to explore fully the potential of the Web for their language learning. Furthermore, it highlights the need for comprehensive staff training to ensure that students are made aware of the technology at their disposal.

Electronic resources: CALL packages

Whereas languages staff have not yet developed a bank of Web-based language learning resources, staff have been at the fore in developing local CALL packages. Staff in French, in particular, have been instrumental in CALL development since the mid-1980s. At that time, a number of languages colleagues obtained funding from the UK-based CTI (Computers in Teaching Initiative) project and the TELL (Technology-Enhanced Language Learning) consortium, based at the University of Hull, to design packages. Three CALL programs, designed using HyperCard, were subsequently produced: *TAP*, *MetaText* and *MCQ* (Multiple Choice Questions – a *HyperCard* stack used to provide students with banks of multiple choice grammar questions and tests). Each package fits neatly onto a floppy disk and is not centrally run from a server. *TAP* and *MetaText*, in particular, have been used in textual analysis and translation classes for second year students of French on the four main undergraduate language degree programmes at Coleraine and Magee. The *TAP* package was removed from the International Business Communication at Magee after the installation of a new PC-platform Faculty computing lab on that campus in 1999. *MCQ* has not been extensively used in recent years and comprehensive banks of grammar questions have not yet been developed for it. A version of *MetaText* has been created for PC, although some modifications are to be made before it is introduced to students.

Spanish, too, has been involved in the creation of local CALL programs: in 1996, a lecturer and one of the Faculty technicians developed a self-correcting Mac-based grammar package, using the *Authorware* shell, naming it *OLE*. The package was piloted among several students but has never been completely developed and is not currently available to students. It may never become fully operational unless it can work on a PC platform.

In 1999, the School of Languages and Literature, as part of the TELL consortium, was able to acquire a number of commercially available CALL packages, including *TransIT Tiger* and the grammar testing software, *GramEx* and *GramDef*. These packages have never been used since they are PC-platform based and, until recently, most staff and students were using Macintosh machines. Consequently, few staff had the opportunity to develop exercises or other course material to be used with these packages.

The University does not have a very comprehensive bank of CALL resources. One of the main reasons why developments in this area have been slow has been the use of a Mac instead of a PC platform, which seems to have been adopted by many CALL developers as the normal platform. The decision to create CALL exercises on *Campus One* system, though, shows an interest in developing Web-based language-learning material. Such material is not platform dependent and therefore reduces the problem of compatibility, which hindered CALL development at Ulster in recent years.

Results from the staff questionnaire revealed that CALL packages are not widely used at the University. Only one member of staff currently uses CALL and also encourages students to use it for private study. This is a surprising revelation considering the School of Language and Literature's involvement in CALL initiatives since the mid 1980s, especially the development of in-house packages. The main reason for this limited use of CALL for teaching is that since the University moved away from using the Mac platform, it is now almost impossible to access most of the in-house CALL packages. Furthermore, since there are few packages available at Ulster and since some of the packages are only suited for use in certain types of classes, such as textual analysis and translation, this limits the potential use for such programs. Consequently, successful integration of CALL into the languages curriculum appears not to be a reality – a view shared by Gillespie and McKee (1999b: 452). Staff may also be mindful of the resistance that students have expressed about using *MetaText* and *TAP* in previous years (Gillespie and McKee (1999a: 38–42)). As a result, tutors seem reluctant to use these programs or even to try new packages.

Of course, even if staff do not use CALL in class, there is no reason why they cannot encourage students to use them for private study. The apparent unwillingness to do this contrasts with the overwhelming endorsement by staff of the Web, with over 70% encouraging students to use it for private study. Many staff want their students to use the computer as part of their self-study activities, although that does not seem to include CALL. This reveals an important finding: staff will encourage students to use the computer in their language learning if they believe it is beneficial to students. This does not mean that staff feel CALL is not beneficial, but probably suggests that many have little experience of such packages and do not appreciate their value. On the other hand, many staff use the Web everyday, including for their own research, and therefore have a clearer understanding of its pedagogical value. If staff are unfamiliar or unsure of something, they can hardly be expected to recommend it to their students. This highlights the need to make staff aware of CALL packages and related activities that are available to them.

Results from the student questionnaires reflect those of staff. 11% of students admitted using CALL. Of the eight students who use CALL, 38% said they use it for class-related activities (*MetaText*, for example), the same percentage use these packages for private study and 18% use it for both. Given that there is little evidence of staff encouraging students to use it for private study, this finding is hardly unexpected. This suggests that there is little sign of a CALL ethos at Ulster, which supports Gillespie and McKee's view (1999a: 45) that independent learning with CALL at Ulster does not happen. There are, however, a number of other reasons that explain why CALL is not widely used by students.

- Firstly, students, like staff, are not always aware of the potential of CALL packages. The comments of first year students in their questionnaires show a lack of knowledge about CALL: 'There aren't a lot of language learning packages available…never knew that there were language learning packages available.' Some second year students in one of the focus group sessions did not know what CALL programs were. Many will probably remain ignorant about CALL unless staff show them the types of packages available and recommend their use.
- Secondly, it is used in isolation. *MetaText*, for example, is normally only used by second year students in French for one semester. It is never used after that point. As a result, students begin to question its relevance in their course. *MetaText* is an electronic translation and vocabulary workbook, which is used to encourage students to work entirely on-screen. It was expected to be used in conjunction with on-line or server-based dictionaries, although in reality many students tend not to do this (the Mac/PC compatibility problem meant that as a Mac-based application, it was not possible to link *MetaText* into the served-based French dictionaries, running on PC). In other words, the use of *MetaText* seems to have led students to think that the computer is just being used for the sake of it, without any clear pedagogical advantage,

which was not the intention of the package or its designers. Final year students expressed this view during a focus group session.

If students feel that something is beneficial, resistance towards using it diminishes. Evidence of this can be seen in the case of the recent French, Spanish and German Web-based grammar diagnostic tests that students at Coleraine completed. First and fourth year students undertook the test – because of time constraints, the finalists were asked to complete them in their own time. Twenty-one out of the twenty-five final years who were asked to do the test, completed it within the initial one-week time limit they were set. Three more completed it before the end of the extended time limit, one week later. One student, who was not shown how to access the tests nor initially asked to complete them, e-mailed the tutor responsible for it, expressing a strong desire to complete the French test. Subsequent feedback, based on discussions with the students, has revealed that students were generally enthusiastic about the tests and considered them to be valuable. They were used to assess the level of final year grammar, allowing tutors to focus on deficient areas in optional remedial grammar classes. The final years who completed the tests were very keen to evaluate their performance and to understand where they went wrong, indicating a strong desire to focus on their grammar proficiency, due probably to the fact that this area is not systemically studied in the final year French curriculum. As a result, students could see an obvious advantage for using computer technology in their language learning. In addition, it appears that, since the tests were Web-based, this played an important role in enhancing their popularity because it gave the students the flexibility to complete them anywhere and at any time. Nevertheless, in the absence of quantitative analysis or a comparative test completed on a local client-based CALL program, it is difficult to prove the success of these tests definitively.

The attitudes of staff and students towards the Web and CALL packages show that whereas the Web has been globally adopted at Ulster as a reliable and essential source of information, there is less conviction about the use of CALL. If staff and students were more aware of the value of CALL, had a more comprehensive understanding of the types of packages available to them and felt that they had a role in their language learning and teaching, (perhaps through training sessions or workshops or even a regularly updated directory of resources, along the lines of a booklist, for example), they may be more willing to use it.

Computer labs for languages

On both the Coleraine and Magee campuses, languages students have access to a Faculty of Arts computing lab. The Magee lab provides fifteen PCs, while the lab in Coleraine has twenty-five workstations. Both these labs are located within a short distance of the offices of languages staff and main teaching rooms. They are open each weekday from early morning until 10.00pm. They are used by staff and students from all schools and subjects in the Faculty. The Coleraine lab is normally closed for teaching purposes between four and five hours per day, allowing students open access to these labs at all other times, including Saturdays. Even if the labs are closed, at weekends, for example, students can ask the on-site security staff to open them. In addition to these labs, the students at Coleraine have access to a second, smaller Faculty computing lab, in the médiathèque, which until the end of the 2001/02 academic year, contained twenty Power or Performa Macintosh machines. Although not exclusive to languages students, in practice, the médiathèque computer lab has normally been used only by them. Until 2001/02, this lab was one of the few remaining Macintosh rooms in the entire University – the main Faculty labs at Coleraine and Magee were Mac-based until conversion to PC and are now part of the IT User Services corporate lab system. The hardware and software in the médiathèque lab was not as modern as in the PC Faculty labs. This meant that these computers were effectively isolated from parts of the University network, including the Common Desktop Environment and access to student e-mail servers and accounts. Like the larger PC rooms, this lab was open access, until 10.00pm. The médiathèque lab was rarely occupied for teaching purposes: exceptionally, during the first semester of 2000/01, it was closed for teaching an average of two hours per week. As a result, students had virtually uninterrupted open access to this lab.

Before their conversion to PC, the main Faculty labs at Coleraine and Magee were used for teaching *TAP* and *MetaText* as part of the French course. Students would use the lab to complete weekly translations using *MetaText*. Until 1996, texts for new translations to be completed on *MetaText* were added to students' floppy disks in a laborious and time-consuming process of copying and pasting files from the tutor's source disk or selected hard drives. Similarly, students' translations had to be printed out or copied onto a spare disk and submitted to the tutor. After that period, when *FirstClass* was introduced, the procedure was simplified and greatly speeded up. Texts were then sent through *FirstClass* to students, who would paste them into the *MetaText* stack on disk. Likewise, when students completed translations or class tests, they were required to submit them electronically to the tutor, using *FirstClass*. He would then correct their scripts on-screen and return them to the students who, in turn, would copy and paste the corrected translations from *FirstClass* into their *MetaText* notebook for examination revision purposes.

Tutors in other languages have used the Faculty computer labs for teaching on both the Magee and Coleraine campuses, although these classes have tended to be induction or explanatory sessions – demonstrating the use of certain software. First year students in Applied Languages take a computer induction module and most of the weekly hourly sessions usually take place in one of the Coleraine Faculty computer labs, giving students hands-on practice using computers and specific software packages.

On both campuses, students have relatively unfettered access to the Faculty computing rooms and these rooms are located in convenient areas for students. Consequently, the Faculty computer labs are used extensively for private study. Furthermore, since most of the buildings on each campus are spread over a small area, even when the main Faculty labs are occupied, it is usually only a short walk for students to use labs in other faculties or in the libraries. Since the University does not yet use an extensive range of language learning programs, the Faculty labs do not run CALL programs. Before their conversion to PC platform, students who had *MetaText* translation or *TAP* classes were required to use the main Faculty labs outside teaching hours to work on their translation assignments and develop their custom glossaries. Students now tend to use the Faculty labs for generic computing purposes, such as typing up assignments, in addition to Web searching, either for personal entertainment or to research material for essays or other coursework. In other words, they use general programs that can be found in all corporate computing labs across the University.

One might think that since the médiathèque computer lab ran older hardware and software and could not access all University network facilities such as e-mail, students would tend not to use it and instead would use the newer PC rooms. Nevertheless, some students, especially modern linguists, would visit it regularly. Students used it to access their *FirstClass* accounts and print off notes, details of coursework or other information using dot matrix printers, which were the only printing facilities available to students free of charge on campus. Students could also use a laser printer for high-quality printing, which used a charge card system like other labs in the University. However, since these computer facilities were almost exclusively used by language students, there were normally fewer queues for this printer and less chance of technical problems or paper shortages than in the main computer labs. In addition, since a large proportion of the language students tend to use Web-based e-mail accounts, such as Yahoo or Hotmail, they could just as easily access their e-mail (except their University accounts) using the old computers in the médiathèque lab as in any of the main corporate labs. Furthermore, these computer facilities were conveniently located beside a private study room, where many students work when not in class.

As each year passed the médiathèque computer lab on the Coleraine campus became more dated and less functional. The 2001/02 academic year saw fewer students using that lab than before. The lab was in need of upgrading and, recognising this, the School of Languages and Literature replaced the computers in that room with state-of-the-art multimedia PCs at the end of the 2001/02 academic year. It is hoped that the multimedia labs will be extended to the other campuses. The labs serve as digital language laboratories, replacing some of the current analogue labs. Each machine is linked to a tutor's workstation, which has control over all the PCs and allows the tutor to chat to students through a headset and even view the students' desktop to facilitate progress monitoring. In addition, each PC is connected to a mini video camera and operates video conferencing software. This allows for distance teaching and, in particular, enables tutors to teach classes across campuses simultaneously. The labs are connected to the main University network, allowing students to access University e-mail accounts and other generic software packages from these rooms. The computers are being installed with CALL packages, links to server-based dictionaries and other language specific material such as digitised audiovisual clips – news broadcasts, for example.

The labs are still being developed, although the obvious purpose of the project is to develop the use of computer technology in language learning at the University and to encourage more staff to use computers in their teaching. Staff and students, though, need to feel there is a need for using computer technology (namely that they see it as pedagogically beneficial), otherwise they seem unwilling to use it. The same could be true of these new computer labs and students and staff will need to be encouraged to use them. Curriculum integration is an important factor in encouraging the use of such facilities and the designers of the languages computer rooms have already considered one way of enhancing curriculum integration. The labs will replace some of the analogue language laboratories. All the language courses in Coleraine, Magee and Belfast include one hour of teaching (any-thing from video comprehension to phonetics and pronunciation exercises) every week in each language module in an analogue lan-guage laboratory. This means that staff will be required to teach in the new digital labs. When they start using the multimedia rooms, staff and students will almost certainly begin exploring some of the other facilities that the multimedia labs provide. This would thereby encour-age staff and students to use these labs for other activities, perhaps even using CALL software.

The languages computer labs might also help address a problem that many students commented upon in the questionnaires – suitable access to facilities. Although languages students will not have ex-clusive access to the labs, they will be given priority. In their ques-tionnaire responses, students remarked that although there were good computing facilities at Ulster (69% felt there were adequate facilities), access was a major problem. One student commented: 'although labs are getting better, access is still limited and it can be difficult to spend any length of time working in a lab without being asked to move.' Languages students at Coleraine and Magee tend to use one or two computer labs because they are convenient to lecture theatres and seminar rooms used for language teaching. The problem arises when these labs are heavily booked for teaching purposes. Students often have to find another computer lab, perhaps located on the other side of campus. This can be problematic for students who have limited time to spare between classes to use computers to type up essays and print off notes. Alternatively, they are forced to wait until later in the day to use the computers, usually after 5.00pm, when it may not suit them to visit the labs. Some students on the Magee campus noted that they were asked to prepare an assignment that required special software, which was only available in one lab, yet this lab was so heavily booked for teaching that they could only use it in the evening. As one student commented on in his questionnaire, if students are expected to use *FirstClass*, e-mail or the Web to communicate with staff or send and receive notes or coursework, they need good access to computers. Poor access will frustrate even the most assiduous student.

Learning approaches

The use of computer technology in learning and teaching at Ulster facilitates both a constructivist and behaviourist approach to learning. The use of *MetaText* and *TAP* within class activities is an example of how the computer is used for both behaviourist and constructivist learning. At the same time, evidence of the constructivist approach can be seen through the way that students are invited to use the Web for self-study. Computer technology has also enabled a combined constructivist-behaviourist approach to learning. The use of grammar diagnostics tests, which feed into teacher-centred grammar classes is one example. Consequently, even though the integration of computers into the language-learning environment is embryonic at Ulster, the technology is being used to facilitate both types of learning approaches

Planning a computer-based language-learning environment

Creating a computer-based language-learning environment involves more than simply using the computer to learn and teach language skills – it needs careful planning and structuring. The extent to which the University has planned to create such an environment is clear in two areas: the role of management in developing the use of computer technology and the level of impetus from academic staff and students for its creation.

Role of management: computer training

Wenger (1996: 58) argues that 'implementing and supporting information technology has such financial implications on campuses that the absence of commitment by senior management ultimately means failure'. Management at Ulster have two main roles in developing a computer-based environment: ensuring that computer technology is central to everyday university life and, secondly, providing support for its creation.

One way of ensuring that the computer is seen as a central and natural part of the university experience is to create a culture in which the computer is seen as so important and essential for even the most basic of tasks that to do without it would be unthinkable. This involves two stages. Firstly, it is important to ensure high levels of computer literacy, in order to make computer technology less of a feared technical obstacle for its users. Secondly, it requires integrating computer technology in key areas of learning and teaching.

In order to make the computer less of an obstacle for those who use it, students and staff often require training to allow them to feel comfortable and competent using computers. As more and more students receive computer training at secondary school and have access to a computer at home, an increasing proportion come to university already very confident using computers. This is, however, not always the case: Martin (1997: 2), for example, believes that all students are not necessarily computer literate when they arrive at university. Staff are probably less likely to be so confident and computer literate. At the University of Ulster, induction and training in the use of computers is available to all students and staff – for those in languages, induction is available at two levels: from IT User Services and from the School of Languages and Literature.

In 1999, IT User Services introduced an eight-week BITS course (Basic Information Technology Skills) that would be available to undergraduate students in all years, although primarily targeting new first year students. This course offers the usual range of training in generic computer applications. Most students opt not to take the BITS course.[1] This may be explained for two reasons: either most students feel this course is too basic and that they have already received similar training at secondary school or, equally, since the course is not a necessary prerequisite for their degree course nor does it offer any kind of accreditation, such as a certificate or other qualification, students may feel that they do not have the time to spend on such a course for little palpable reward.

In the same way, Staff Development Courses are organised to train staff in the basics and more advanced complexities of computer technology. These courses are characterised by relatively poor attendance, probably because of considerable time constraints on staff.

The training mentioned above provides general IT training in a variety of packages. The School however offers more specialised training in the use of packages and techniques for language learning and teaching purposes. Students taking the Applied Languages degree course are required to complete a compulsory twelve-week Information Studies module in their first year of study. The module provides training in using the World Wide Web for language learning, the use of *FirstClass* and some classes on CALL packages. The course has proved very useful for most students who appear to feel more confident using computers after completing it. The module is only available to students on one course, with around twenty students com-

1   According to the BITS annual report for 2000/01 at (Accessed on University Intranet, May 2001) 1000 students from across the four campuses of the University of Ulster and across faculties who took part in it.

pleting it each year. With such a small client base, it is clear that the module and the skills it teaches are not being offered to even a majority of languages students. The other languages students at Coleraine currently receive a more erratic programme of induction. At the beginning of each academic year, these students are now offered an induction session, usually in use of *FirstClass* and any other aspects, such as disk management, that can be crammed into a one-hour session. Whereas this session is obviously open to a substantial proportion of language students (serving a larger client base than the Information Studies module), in practice, few students attend it, usually because the workshop is not compulsory and students are not explicitly encouraged to attend. Languages students on the Jordanstown and Magee campuses do not receive this type of systematic induction and any training provided tends to be *ad hoc*.

School induction sessions for staff are much less systematic than the training offered to students. Each year, sporadic workshops are organised for languages staff. In the 1999/2000 academic year, for example, a workshop was organised by the Head of School to train (and in some cases, re-train) staff in the use of *FirstClass* and it was well attended. One of the difficulties with staff induction sessions at Ulster is that, since staff are based on different campuses, it can be difficult to arrange workshops that will be attended by all staff, including those on other campuses, especially if the workshops are arranged during term-time.

The levels of training available to both groups suggest similar standards of computer literacy. More systematic training for languages staff and students would be useful. Perhaps, however, since few computer-based language learning resources are available at Ulster, the need for extensive training has not seemed that important and will only grow as these facilities are developed.

Role of management: ICT integration

Training students and staff in the use of the computer and making them more competent users, while important in integrating computer technology into a language-learning environment, is not the only way of achieving that goal. Another factor is the successful incorporation of the computer into the University environment, making it a pivotal and central part of everyday life and activities at the University. At Ulster, the computer plays an ever-increasingly important role in the daily life of staff and students. This role is clearly seen in a number of different areas, including the development of a Web-based student records system, an increased variety of electronic library resources and the creation of an on-line learning environment.

IT User Services introduced the Student PIN system, where all students were issued with a unique personal identification number that they would use to activate their e-mail accounts through a facility called the Student Web or UUSIS (University of Ulster Student Information System). The Student Web facility includes a record of students' examination results for each semester, which is accessible across the Web.

It is expected that the Student Web system will gradually contain more student enrolment details, course information and details of outstanding tuition fees, along with other information that students may require access to. From the autumn of 2002, students will be required to enrol for modules or courses using the UUSIS. Staff have access to student records, their enrolment details and other personal information, such as term-time and home addresses, using the Web, on and off-campus. These developments mean that staff and students are increasingly in a position to use the computer to access administrative information with considerable ease.

In addition, University library facilities are quite highly computerised. The institution was one of the first in the UK to operate an electronic catalogue of books, which now includes an on-line book reservation and renewal service. The catalogue also allows users to check borrower information, such as details of book return dates and the cost of any outstanding fines. Furthermore, the Library is developing an electronic loan reminder facility that will send an e-mail message to a student or member of staff just before the return date for books they have borrowed. When introduced, it will replace the circulation of hard copy reminders. When fully introduced, this system will require users to check their e-mail accounts regularly and, in general, rely more on computer technology and less on the conventional methods of library administration. It is an example of the University's desire to promote an increasingly electronic and computer culture among staff and students, requiring even the most technophobic students and staff to embrace the technology.

In addition to the advanced catalogue system, a division of the University Library, known as Electronic Information Services, provides a range of electronic resources, such as CD-ROM databases, dictionaries and citation indexes. Each year, Electronic Information Services spend a total of £150,000 developing these resources. One of the most recent developments has been the creation of a database of previous examination to replace the current hard copy archive system for past papers. In January 2001, the provision of electronic library resources received a much-needed boost with improvements to the Athens Access Management System. Formerly, all staff and students accessed the Athens system with a common password and username and were required to access it using a University PC: as a result, services provided by Athens were quite limited, mainly being used to access the BIDS citation index. Since January 2001, every student and member of staff is issued with a personal username and password (login details are automatically sent to the University e-mail addresses of all incoming students), enabling them to access their Athens accounts on and off-campus. This has led to an increase in the range of resources that can be accessed through Athens, which now includes electronic journals, including language learning periodicals. This provides languages students and staff with global access to material that is normally only held in the libraries on each campus, either for coursework assignments or academic research, without needing to attend campus to obtain the material. The ability to access library resources will be particularly useful for those students who commute to University each day and have limited time to spend in the libraries on campus, in the evening for example. The University intends that by 2010 between 65% and 90% of academic journals held by the Library will be available exclusively in electronic format and that there will be a large quantity of electronic books available by 2008. This means that whether staff and students like it or not, they will need to use computer technology increasingly to access key resources and materials. It is further evidence of the growing e-culture at the University.

During the academic year 2001/02, the University introduced *Campus One*, a virtual learning environment created through *WebCT*. Substantial funding has been provided by the University's Open and Distance Learning (ODL) initiative to set up this system, which will come into operation fully in the 2002/03 academic year. *Campus One* has been designed to provide a range of distance learning courses, although it is intended that the system will also be used by staff and students on campus. It will offer the normal facilities of a Virtual Learning Environment, such as an e-mail facility for contacting course tutors and the ability to post up course notes or send and receive coursework. In addition, *Campus One* will provide unique timetabling information for every student, as well as offering a calendar facility that will allow staff and students to keep track of appointments and assignment deadlines. It will make it easier for staff to publish their course material and notes in Web format since the package is essentially an extranet (externally-accessible intranet), thereby meaning that material made available through it will not be openly available on the Web. This means that staff will not be subject to the Web publishing protocol that has really restricted staff and often prevented interested colleagues from publishing material on the University website in the past. *Campus One* will also link into the UUSIS to enable students to check whether their fees have been paid, along with other student information. All students will be registered automatically on *Campus One* when they enrol in the University for the first time. Whereas certain courses may opt not to use it extensively, or even at all, students and staff will need to use it quite regularly since Academic Registry and the Examinations Office will use the system heavily to post up administrative information.

Campus One offers more possibilities for language learning than would have been possible with *FirstClass*. Audiovisual material can be streamed through *Campus One*, therefore allowing staff to add digitised video or audio clips to course notes or to set on-line assignments, such as listening comprehensions. This will be particularly important in the context of the new languages computer labs. Since the School will need to digitise many hours of news clips and listening comprehensions for use in the languages computer labs, some of this material may be easily made available on *Campus One*.

101

Banks of digitised material can be built up through the *WebCT* system, allowing students to access these clips for self-study purposes on and off-campus. The ability to design on-line tests and exercises through *Campus One* will be an undoubtedly welcome development for the School of Languages and Literature, allowing colleagues to design their own language learning exercises, either developing them for assessment purposes or as a self-study option for students – a process that has already started with the creation of grammar diagnostic tests. The importance of *Campus One* for languages is particularly significant as its arrival coincides with the installation of multimedia language labs, which will have a major impact on the way the computer is used in language learning and teaching at this institution.

Role of management: support

Financial and academic support given by University-wide and School management is important in creating a computer-based environment. If ICT is to become successfully integrated into learning and teaching, good facilities and resources are an obvious necessity and it is normally the responsibility of management to secure funding for these. Within the School of Languages and Literature, facilities are improving. Staff now have better computing facilities in their offices. In addition, the extensive plans to create language computer laboratories on each campus show a clear desire to provide suitable computing facilities for languages students, too. The improvements that are due to be made to these computer facilities will also be enhanced by the *Campus One* initiative. Perhaps if *Campus One* encourages staff to post lecture notes and develop course material in Web format, there will be more demand for good Web publishing facilities and the University may decide to relax its currently restrictive policy in this area.

In spite of improved computing facilities, technical support in languages is lacking. There is one technician for the Faculty of Arts on each campus (two at Coleraine). It is not surprising, therefore, that there are major demands placed on these staff and they are unable to deal with technical problems as efficiently as they would like. Technicians record target language news broadcasts from satellite television onto VHS tapes for use within the Languages Resource Centre or in the language labs. The arrival of the new suite of multimedia language labs will mean that, instead of recording target language material onto VHS, it will be digitised. This will add more pressure to the technical staff because, unlike at the moment where teaching staff can delve into a bank of pre-recorded VHS tapes of target language material to prepare tests or language lab activities, it will take time to create a bank of digitised material and archives that currently does not exist. One possible solution to this may come from the Institute of Lifelong Learning, which is responsible for assisting academic staff in the process of preparing course material for use on *Campus One*. These support staff may be able to digitise audiovisual material for academic staff on request. It is obvious, however, that unless adequate support staff are provided by the School, Faculty or at institutional level, the responsibility for preparing digitised material and other forms of courseware will rest with academics. Since there are often considerable time constraints on academic staff, engaged both in research and teaching, many will not have time to prepare this material and others may not have suitable technical skills to do so.

If staff are expected to spend long periods of time preparing computer-based courseware or converting lecture notes to electronic format, it is not unreasonable for them to expect some kind of academic credit for doing so. This may take the form of giving sabbaticals to staff to allow them to develop courseware or prepare course material in electronic format, rather than expecting them to do so alongside their other teaching and administrative duties. This would also allow interested staff to use their courseware as a basis for research and seek publications in the area of CALL and language pedagogy, for example. The attitude of management at Ulster towards staff involved in the area of computer-based language learning is unambiguous. Work in this area is given due recognition. Perhaps one significant sign of this was the University decision in 1999 to appoint a senior academic who has been very active in this area of research, including developing his own CALL packages, to the position of Head of the School of Languages and Literature. This has enhanced the profile of CALL and ICT within the School: articles on computer-based language learning were submitted in the 2001 Research Assessment Exercise (RAE). Furthermore, a centre for Research in Applied Languages at the University has been created. In addition to promoting research in area studies and language, the Centre will be involved in developing ICT projects and furthering computer-based language learning.

Since the appointment of a Head of School with a keen interest in using ICT in language learning, a clear ICT policy has been developed. E-mail is now almost exclusively used for official School memos, minutes of meetings and other information and hard copy versions of this material is only provided on request. In 1999/2000, the School adopted the policy of using electronic communication between staff as much as possible and to consolidate the use of *First-Class* for staff-student communication. As a result, the numbers of staff using *FirstClass* that year almost doubled, compared to the previous year (15 in 1999/2000, compared with 8 in 1998/99).

Prior to the appointment of its current Head, the School of Languages and Literature appointed an Open Language Learning Advisor, part of whose responsibility was to advise students on research methodology, including directing them in using the Web for research and developing a short directory of valuable language websites for all the languages taught within the School. This post was funded by the SMILE project (Strategies for Managing Independent Learning Environments). Funding for the advisor, though, was limited and was exhausted by the middle of the 2000/01 academic year: the post has since been suspended.

Support from the chalk face

Ultimately, a computer-based environment will fail unless those who are expected to use the technology (academic staff and students) believe in its value. The level of grassroots support for it can be seen in the attitudes of staff and students towards its value in learning and teaching.

Questionnaire results showed that staff are generally enthused by the use of ICT. 62% of respondents (N=13) felt that its use encourages students to engage in more independent study, especially through the use of the Web and CALL software. Only 8% felt that it had a negative impact on the level of independent study among their students. Staff also seem aware of the value that ICT brings to language learning and teaching. This view is supported by the comments of staff who were asked if they felt that the use of ICT was beneficial or detrimental to the process of student learning. Many expressed the view that its use is a welcome development in the process of student learning. Although positive in their outlook, most respondents stated that the benefits it offers are conditional on other factors, such as sensible integration into mainstream teaching. In other words, they believe in using it because it is beneficial and vital to the process of student learning, and not using it for the sake of it. Comments from staff also showed that ICT ought to be used in conjunction with other resources, such as existing library facilities, and to support current pedagogy. It would seem that staff feel the use of ICT might become excessive and that would lead to changes in teaching and learning that are not necessary or helpful. This highlights the importance of ensuring that the increased use of computer technology is driven by need.

Students too were generally enthusiastic about using ICT and many expressed the view that it is beneficial to their language learning. Student questionnaire responses showed that, whereas many saw merit to using computer technology, they felt that ICT is not being used to its full potential in the process of learning and teaching. One student asked for better training to be provided. Comments made by students in their questionnaires, as well as views expressed at focus group sessions, showed that many students did not know how to use the Web more effectively for researching material – few knew about the gateways for Web resources in French, German and Spanish offered at Ulster and at many other institutions throughout the world. One student remarked that finding suitable research material on the Web was just potluck! These findings show the necessity for suitable training for students in the use of the Web and computer-based resources, such as dictionaries and CALL packages. Furthermore, given that resources change continually and new facilities become available, it is important that sustained and regular training is needed to make students aware of the evolving resources and facilities that are continually becoming available to them.

The student questionnaires showed an overwhelmingly positive attitude towards the Web. Many cited the ability to access up-to-date information quickly through it as an obvious advantage, in spite of the occasional difficulties experienced trying to find relevant information easily. Similarly, there were encouraging comments made about *First-Class*. Despite the fact that this system has recently proved itself to be slightly unreliable and students are regularly unable to access their accounts using the Web interface because of server outages, many students remained generally enthused by the system. Only two students expressed disappointment with the unreliability of *FirstClass*. These comments reveal that students are not necessarily discouraged from using technology that is not always reliable and can often prove frustrating. They can see through the technical difficulties and obstacles if the advantages of using technology (such as accessing lecture notes quickly, submitting coursework from home or finding valuable target language material or up-to-date research material) outweigh the disadvantages. This view is supported by Burnage (2001: 169), who explains a similar experience with students at the University of Cambridge. They continue to use this program because of its clear design and layout, in addition to an extensive range of exercises, which shows that students tend to use computer technology because they appreciate its academic value and are less influenced by its appearance or technical superiority.

Chapter Four
Example 2: the University of Cambridge

Background information

As one of the oldest and most famous universities in the world, Cambridge needs little introduction.

History

The University of Cambridge is composed of thirty-one autonomous colleges, many of which have been in existence for hundreds of years: the oldest college is Peterhouse, founded in 1284, whilst the youngest is Robinson College, created in 1977. Although the colleges are separate entities, they are an inseparable part of the University: while the central University body organises lectures and examinations and controls the faculties, the colleges admit students (of which there are approximately twenty thousand full-time and part-time) and look after certain aspects of teaching; they also provide accommodation for their students and organise a wide range of non-academic pursuits for them, including sports, to encourage them to integrate into University life. It is unusual for students not to live in their college accommodation – most will live in college halls of residence (there are over fifteen thousand places). Some colleges do not have enough space in their halls of residence and they rent out houses and flats, normally to finalists and postgraduates.

Students live and work in their colleges during term time. Although they attend lectures and other classes arranged through the central faculty, they have regular classes in their college – these classes are normally small group supervision sessions with three to five students and one tutor: classes in college therefore tend to be very intimate and there is obviously a close relationship between students and college tutors. Some colleges provide excellent facilities like comprehensive libraries and good computing and sporting facilities: most even have their own student bar! As a result, they form a central and intimate part of student life at Cambridge, and it is clear that students identify more with their college (normally spending most of their time there) than with any faculty. The colleges are widely dispersed across the city, and students are therefore based all over the city.

Modern languages at Cambridge – MML Faculty

The Faculty of Modern and Medieval Languages (MML) is responsible for specialist degree-level language courses in twelve languages, including French, Spanish, German, Modern Greek and Russian. There are one hundred and forty-six teaching staff in the seven departments that make up the Faculty (French, German, Italian, Spanish and Portuguese, Other Languages, Slavonic Studies and Linguistics), teaching some eight hundred undergraduate and postgraduate students. Most members of staff, in addition to teaching languages at faculty level, are members or fellows of colleges. Approximately fifty of the MML staff are College Teaching Officers, responsible for language classes in the colleges only: these teaching officers are employed by colleges, and not the University, although they form part of the MML Faculty. The MML Faculty is located inside the Raised Faculty Building (RFB) on the Sidgwick site of the School of Arts and Humanities, beside Selwyn and Newnham colleges. The RFB contains a number of seminar-type teaching rooms where students have classes once or twice a week and the MML library, although the building is really used for administration. Due to constraints in office space, few staff have offices in the RFB – most will be based in an office in their college. Staff, like the students, are therefore dispersed across the city, and some do not even know other colleagues in the Faculty.

Modern Languages teaching in the Faculty provides a wide curriculum, ranging from linguistics to literature studies. Students in years one and two (Tripos Part IA and B) have one hour per week of 'Use of French/German/Spanish…' (language classes), where activities are varied – anything from oral work to grammar or video comprehension. In addition, students in final year (Tripos Part II) do not take these type of language classes but have one hour of translation work once a week or at least every two weeks and target language essay writing classes each week. In addition to these Faculty language classes, colleges will arrange oral/aural classes for their language students. It would seem, though that there are fewer language classes available to MML students than on offer in other institutions, such as Ulster. This reduced emphasis on language work has a significant influence over the way that the computer is used in language teaching and learning and in staff and student perception of its value.

Modern languages at Cambridge – the Cambridge Language Centre

Whereas the MML Faculty is responsible for degree-level language courses, the Language Centre (which is currently located on the Sidgwick site of the University, adjacent to the MML Faculty) is responsible for non-specialist language teaching and non-Faculty languages. A separate body from the Faculty of Modern and Medieval Languages, with its own staff of language teachers and advisors, its main role is to support language teaching throughout the University and provide teaching and learning resources for the language programmes taught there. It offers a wide range of material in over one hundred different languages and supporting over one thousand five hundred learners annually (Esch and Zähner 2000: 14). The Centre provides taught language courses as well as self-study resources for the non-specialist linguists: one of the main courses on offer is the CULP (Cambridge University Language Programme) that is currently being piloted by the Language Centre as a distance language learning course.

Language learning and teaching is therefore taught by two separate bodies, each of which has quite a different focus on their language courses – one teaches language for more practical and less specialised purposes; the other has a more specialised, academic approach. As a result, each body makes use of the computer for language learning and teaching in different ways. However, in order to ensure a balanced comparison between each of the universities examined in this investigation, this chapter will consider the learning and teaching activities of the MML Faculty, although certain parallels and comparisons with those of the Language Centre will be made.

Computer infrastructure

The infrastructure in Cambridge has an important influence on the use of computer technology in learning and teaching.

Computer provision and management

Cambridge is a very disparate and widespread institution and this diversity is reflected at most levels of the University: computer services, for example, are provided by an assortment of different bodies. It can be divided into three parts: the University Computing Service (UCS), which has responsibility for general computer provision in the University, especially networking and e-mail; faculty-level computer technicians, who are responsible for the maintenance and purchase of computing facilities in faculty buildings, especially in staff offices and faculty computer labs, and finally College Computing Officers who are responsible for computing and networking provision in colleges.

The standard of computer provision varies from college to college: some, like Queen's, Trinity and Churchill Colleges have quite modern facilities and multiple computing rooms; others, like King's and Girton seem to have less extensive facilities. Some colleges provide more comprehensive computer resources than others, including separate intranets and e-mail systems. The diversity of facilities is a direct result of the differing financial investment that they are each prepared or able to provide for computing facilities. Increasingly, however, colleges are beginning to enlist the support of the UCS to assist with college computer provision. This can be seen in the provision of the Public Workstation Facility (PWF) Managed Cluster arrangement. The PWF is a common personalised desktop facility, providing students with a generic platform of computer programs and their personal server space. The UCS operates five PWF labs for general purpose computing. They have now begun converting some college computing rooms to PWF (known as the Managed Cluster arrangement) and, rather than being managed by the college, the UCS manage the hardware and software in those rooms for an annual fee.

PWF Managed Clusters are also being set up in a number of faculty computer rooms. Faculty Computing Officers, like their college counterparts, have considerable autonomy: they, rather than the UCS, are responsible for the computer provision in the faculty.

Whereas the PWF has led to greater uniformity of software, in particular, across colleges and faculties, the different levels of computer services means that quite often there is a lack of uniformity between the computing facilities provided by the UCS and faculties and those provided by the colleges. This makes it very difficult to draw overall conclusions about the standard of computer provision at Cambridge and how conducive it is to computer-based learning and teaching and to the creation of a computer-based learning environment.

Networking infrastructure

Given the diverse nature of computing services, it is not surprising that there is a labyrinth of different networks. UCS operates a high-speed network backbone called the *CUDN* (Cambridge University Data Network) that has been installed by the Computing Service in all faculty and University buildings, although not in college buildings. Colleges are responsible for funding the installation of the *CUDN* in their rooms. Some colleges, like Queen's for example, charge a monthly or quarterly fee to students who wish to use the *CUDN*, partly to pay for the initial installation costs of the network. Some colleges, such as Trinity and Churchill, run their own intranet, linked to the *CUDN*. Overall, the number of students who have access to the *CUDN* from their college bedroom is considerable and continues to grow as more of them acquire their own PCs or laptops.

For those students who live in college flats or houses, instead of college halls of residence, networking connections are not always available because these flats and houses may be not be located within the college grounds. For those students, along with staff who do not live in their college, the UCS provides a dial-up service, called *Magpie*, costing £30 for two hundred and fifty hours on-line. Although, like many commercial ISPs, users of *Magpie* pay the cost of a local telephone call to use the service, it provides users with a Cambridge user domain, giving users access to files and websites that are only available on the University intranet. An agreement made with the local telecommunications company, NTL, has allowed staff and post-graduates to subscribe to a telephone exchange service called CU2S that provides them with an internal university extension to their home telephone (or telephone in a college flat): using this service, users can dial into the *CUDN* without paying the cost of a local telephone call. The networking infrastructure at Cambridge is therefore well advanced and students and staff have access to resources and facilities across the *CUDN* both in faculty buildings and computer rooms, as well as their own bedrooms or flat/house, giving them round the clock access to electronic resources and facilities.

E-mail infrastructure

Since many staff and students have flexible access to University network facilities, this allows them to access e-mail accounts and the Web from their accommodation. Given the dispersed nature of Cambridge, quick and efficient communication is vital and e-mail has become an essential means of communication for staff and students. Formerly, the bulk of correspondence within the University and between colleges was carried out by post, using the internal mail service, however, due to the large bulk of mail being sent, the service was not very efficient – letters and memos could take two to three days to be delivered to staff and students across the city. Since e-mail is now used for general correspondence, this has allowed the mail service to become more efficient and letters and other correspondence delivered through it arrive much quicker than before.

Every student is automatically issued with an e-mail account when he or she registers at the University for the first time. Although some colleges, like King's and Selwyn, provide their own e-mail servers and user domains, the vast majority of e-mail accounts are issued and managed centrally by UCS. Before the start of each academic year, the University Computing Service generates e-mail lists for each faculty, containing the e-mail addresses of new students. These lists are sent to each faculty, where they may be divided up into departmental lists.

UCS is researching a number of different webmail systems to provide flexible access to e-mail accounts from anywhere, although, given that most students and staff at Cambridge live locally, either in college residences or a flat (or house), where they can easily access the *CUDN*, they currently have very good and flexible access to their e-mail accounts. This shows that Cambridge has a comprehensive e-mail infrastructure in place. Considering that effective communication has been established as an important part of any learning environment, this would suggest that the Cambridge system is conducive to the development of a computer-based learning environment.

Computer-based language-learning in action

In recent years, the Faculty of Modern and Medieval Languages has invested significantly in computer technology. The Faculty uses computer technology in the process of language learning and teaching in three key areas: facilitating staff-student communication, providing electronic language learning and teaching resources and integrating ICT into class and self-study activities through the use of a CALL Facility. Information has been drawn from questionnaire findings and interviews with students and staff. Questionnaire responses were received from eighty-two students and forty-two members of staff: both sets of questionnaires were administered electronically. Interviews were conducted with nine members of staff in the MML Faculty and with eight undergraduate students.

Electronic communication

The Faculty of Modern and Medieval Languages has become one of the main users of e-mail for internal communication: it is a Faculty way of life. Students are advised to check their e-mail at least twice daily because academic or secretarial staff will send administrative information electronically, such as changes to the time and venue of classes or information about courses. Students on their year abroad are encouraged to use e-mail to communicate with their tutors and submit dissertation drafts and plans. The Faculty has created e-mail distribution lists, divided into year groups, and departmental secretaries create local distribution lists enabling them and the academic staff to send messages to students in that department only: these lists are also divided into year groups. The Spanish and Portuguese department has piloted an electronic registration procedure for paper choices (at Cambridge, students do not take modules, instead they enrol for papers e.g. SP1, 2, 3 etc). Using *E-Form* software, students in Tripos Part IA are sent an e-mail request during the summer vacation to register their paper choices for Tripos IB, using an on-line registration form. Students who do not do so are automatically reminded by e-mail. In the 2000/01 academic year, all students (fifty in total) had completed the registration form by mid-July, allowing timetable arrangements and other administrative details to be finalised long before the beginning of the academic year. This return rate shows that students access their e-mail during the summer vacation. This is confirmed by the results of the student questionnaire, which discovered that 84% of them (N=82, unless otherwise stated) have access to the Internet at home.

E-mail is used as the principal means of staff communication too. All staff use e-mail for administration, to send and receive memos and minutes of meetings for example. Each academic year, staff receive two large bundles of documents in hard copy, including course prospectuses: apart from this, very little other material is sent in hard copy.

There is evidence of an e-mail culture among MML staff and students and this can be seen in two areas: in 1999, the Faculty conducted a survey among its students. This survey was conducted, for the first time, using E-Form. There was a 60% return rate (N=584) and the report into the findings of the questionnaire commented that the use of electronic forms and automatic e-mail reminders greatly boosted its return rate. Similarly, a questionnaire was sent by e-mail to staff and students as part of this present study. It was felt that this was the most effective and quickest way of reaching the majority of students and staff and this was reflected in the return rate. Within one hour of the questionnaire being sent, thirty students had replied by e-mail and after four hours, this figure had risen to sixty. In the case of staff, too, the return rate was greatly enhanced by the use of e-mail, with just below thirty responses two days after the questionnaire was sent. Although there is no quantitative evidence to confirm this, it is difficult to imagine that the return rate would have been higher or even the same if hard copy surveys had been used.

According to the findings of the staff questionnaire, e-mail is used extensively by teaching colleagues in MML: 95% of staff respondents (where N=42, unless stated otherwise) use e-mail regularly for university-related tasks. There are signs that this e-mail culture has influenced staff use of e-mail outside work, with 85% of them making frequent use of this means of communication for corresponding with friends and family.

Many staff use e-mail for three main purposes: 95% communicate with students regularly through it, the same percentage use it to communicate with colleagues and a reduced, although nevertheless high, percentage (79%) send and receive administrative documentation to and from secretarial staff electronically. Despite this high usage of e-mail, it would appear that fewer staff use it to support their teaching methods. Considerably smaller numbers of teaching staff use this medium to send and receive coursework to and from students: 31% of respondents use it to send coursework details, while 33% use it to receive coursework from students. The low percentage in the last question was supported by the results from several interviews and additional comments made by staff on their questionnaires. In the opinion of many colleagues, it is time-consuming, expensive and an unnecessary use of their time to allow students to submit their work electronically, requiring members of staff to print out and collate the work from several students – a member of the German department made this view clear in her questionnaire: 'I don't see why I should print out their [the students' essays] for them.' Of course, it is not necessary to print out work that is sent by e-mail in order to mark it: it can be marked on-screen. Incidence of this method of marking is very limited and only one member of MML staff has adopted a method of marking work on-screen, correcting students' work within e-mail messages, for example. Another reason that may help to explain the reluctance of staff to receive or even send work to students is that students have regular small group supervision sessions with members of staff and it may well be easier to give out work details during those sessions, where students have the opportunity to ask questions or seek clarification face to face with their tutors. The questionnaire findings suggest that staff are willing to use e-mail when they believe it is practical to do so: it is certainly more time efficient for most of them to communicate with colleagues, students and secretarial staff. On the other hand, however, the use of e-mail for teaching activities, such as receiving work from students, is seen as a less efficient use of their time. This supports the view expressed in chapter 3, section 3.4 that computer technology is embraced when it is considered to be beneficial, not just pedagogically but also practically.

The opinions expressed by MML students on the use of e-mail differed considerably from those of staff. According to the questionnaire administered to students, 96% use e-mail regularly for University-related tasks and the same percentage use it for personal tasks. One reason for such a high level of e-mail usage seems to be good access to the Internet: 59% of respondents confirmed they have access to the University *CUDN* (giving access to Web and e-mail facilities) from their college bedrooms. Whereas the percentage of staff and students who use e-mail for University tasks is comparable, a higher proportion of staff use e-mail for truly academic purposes than students. Evidence of this can be found in the results of the next question, which asked students how they used e-mail. 91% of them use e-mail to communicate with friends throughout the University, while 74% use it to communicate with staff and 16% send coursework by e-mail. Student use of e-mail is therefore not confined to academic communication but rather they see its wider appeal. This seems to suggest that students are attracted to e-mail, perhaps due to the fact that they have grown up with it in secondary school and feel very comfortable using it.

There are a number of factors that may help to explain why e-mail is used more for general communication by staff and students and less as an integral part of learning and teaching in the MML Faculty: staff reluctance to accept and administer e-mailed work is the most obvious, in addition to the high level of student-tutor personal contact at this university, not least the small group supervision sessions. Another important reason is the tendency of students to submit handwritten rather than word-processed work. Following discussions with some students and staff, it became clear that submitting handwritten work, especially essays, is advocated and preferred to material prepared on word-processor because it is considered more appropriate in training students in linear writing and cognitive techniques and hence more beneficial for students when they complete timed essays in their examinations. Some members of staff require students to submit handwritten work throughout the year (except for final year dissertations, which must be word-processed), whilst others encourage them to submit this type of work near examination periods; consequently, many students become more accustomed to submitting handwritten work than word-processed material. During an interview with one French lecturer, he confirmed that approximately 10% of the work he receives from his students is word-processed; whilst in a sample of Spanish translations submitted to the departmental secretary, ten out of fourteen were handwritten. In view of the clear preponderance of handwritten work, it is quite obvious that, in many cases, electronic submission of work would be impractical. It is, however, not completely redundant: a number of tutors admitted in their questionnaires that they would accept e-mailed work in exceptional cases. In one incidence, a French tutor based at Girton College confirmed that she accepted e-mailed work from many of her students because she felt that it proved too awkward for students to travel to this college to submit work because it is located approximately three miles out of the city and would necessitate students making a round trip of forty minutes to one hour. Whereas students in the MML Faculty of Cambridge have between fourteen and eighteen hours of classes per week, comparable to modern languages students at other institutions, such as Ulster, considerable time is lost travelling between classes in different buildings and colleges. Further time is lost submitting work in person, outside class or supervision hours, for example. The use of e-mail therefore seems a more time-efficient way of submitting work. This view could be widely held by many students, although there is little evidence from student questionnaires to support this – only one student discussed the benefits of electronic work submission in his questionnaire.

Given the apparent culture of handwritten work that exists in Cambridge, it is difficult to see how e-mail could be used integrated further into the teaching and learning experience of the Faculty nor is there much evidence to suggest that staff and students are particularly keen to change the *status quo*. It seems that, unless this culture undergoes radical change, the role of e-mail in the language-learning environment at Cambridge will remain one of an electronic information noticeboard.

Language students have access to a wide range of computer-based resources and these are provided by two principal sources: the MML Faculty and the Language Centre.

MML Electronic resources: the World Wide Web

In 1996, the MML Faculty board appointed a full-time Computer-Assisted Language-Learning (CALL) Officer who is directly responsible to the CALL co-ordinator (a full-time lecturer). One of the duties of the CALL Officer is to assist teaching staff in their preparation of electronic material, in an effort to integrate computer technology into teaching activities. Since his appointment, a number of resources have been designed and built up, ranging from Web-based material to locally networked CALL packages.

As part of his duties, the CALL Officer has shown a number of staff how to publish material on the Web. He was also involved in creating the Faculty website. That site contains general administrative information for courses in the MML Faculty, including dissertation guidelines, advice and guidelines about the Year Abroad, a directory of MML staff contact details and links to on-line material provided by staff on their own websites as well as external Web-based resources in each language.

Staff in the department of Spanish and Portuguese, in particular, have begun to publish material on the Web, ranging from gap-filling exercises to course websites. Two members of staff use these course sites to provide resources for their classes. In the 2000/01 academic year, one of them used his website for the first time to convey information to his students taking Spanish Paper five (which, in comparison to other language classes at Cambridge, had a large group of students – twenty-six in total), publishing supervision timetables, administrative information, lecture handouts, as well as providing links to Spanish Web resources and lecture notes on occasions. Periodically, he also publishes lecture outline and backup notes (including digitised video clips, dealing with aspects of Spanish theatre) on the Web for his students taking other Spanish papers, and has created a bank of annotated translations, in HTML format that work along the lines of *TransIT Tiger*.

One of his colleagues has designed a Web-based grammar survival kit for Romance languages, including a glossary of linguistic grammatical terms. He has also designed on-line translation activities and provides a bank of password-protected texts to be studied in Spanish Papers one and two. All these texts are available in the Cambridge University Libraries but copies are limited and usually in high demand.

Two members of the Spanish department have embarked upon an ambitious pilot project for video comprehension. These two colleagues are in the process of digitising a bank of video clips, with support from the Language Centre and the CALL Officer. Some of these clips will be used as mock video comprehension exam papers. They experimented with the idea of replacing video comprehension classes in the 2000/01 academic year with a series of digitised video clips, which

119

students watched in their own time. This freed up that class for other language-learning activities. The tutors sent the corresponding questions for each video comprehension to their students electronically, either by e-mail, or through a Web page or, alternatively, distributed photocopied handouts of the questions.

The Spanish and Portuguese department seems to be leading the way in the production of systematic Web-based material, followed by the department of Slavonic Studies and particularly Russian Studies. In this department, one tutor has designed a course website for students taking Russian Papers one and four. This website includes HTML versions of set texts and links to Russian websites as well as English sites that provide useful historical and cultural information for topics covered in class. Furthermore, the site provides material for prose classes, including vocabulary hints for set proses.

Other departments offer Web-based material on an unsystematic and more limited basis, including translation exercises, usually produced by the CALL Officer on request by a member of the teaching staff, for use within class. This type of material is often produced for a one-off class activity rather than used recurrently.

When asked in their questionnaire how they used the Web, tutors cited two uses in particular: 57% use it regularly for researching material for class, such as newspaper and journal articles, and 69% said they use it for academic research (in all cases, N=42). Only 17% frequently use it to present lecture notes and other class material, while 14% have designed CALL exercises on the Web. In other words, their usage of the Web is more passive than active – preferring to use it to consult other material already published, rather than using it to publish their own material. This is another sign of the reference library culture among staff, mentioned in Chapter 3. It shows that much of the interactive language learning and teaching potential is really lost on many tutors. All staff have the right to publish material through the University website and the UCS issues passwords to all staff to give them access to the Web servers. In the MML Faculty, the CALL Officer distributes these passwords on request and, at the time of writing, approximately one quarter of the staff had requested passwords from him. There are at least two reasons why more staff do not use the Web for publishing material, both of which are closely related. Staff have not taken up their passwords and begun using the Web to publish material because they are unsure how to do so and this lack of knowledge or confidence about using the Web is due to a lack of training. The second reason that explains why staff tend not to publish on the Web is that, as staff themselves have admitted in their questionnaires and interviews, they simply do not have time to attend training sessions. One tutor remarked that it is 'sometimes hard to fit in extra [computer training] courses with our current demanding schedules.' Time is obviously an issue that all university teaching staff face, not just those at Cambridge. Nevertheless one of the reasons why staff feel so pressurised by time at this institution is that unlike many other universities, at least in the UK, most Faculty staff hold two positions: they teach in the Faculty and in college (as well as supervising students regularly in college and taking on other responsibilities there, such as the post of librarian, admissions officer etc (Burnage 1999: 12). These time pressures mean that even if more training sessions were planned, it would be difficult to arrange these at times convenient for staff.

When asked how they encouraged their students to use the Web in the course of their studies, three activities were highlighted by staff. 55% encourage their students to make regular use of the Web to research topics for essays and other work, while 69% encourage students to access target language material on the Web for self-study purposes. This suggests that a substantial proportion encourage students to use the Web as a source of reference and research, although it seems to be promoted more as a self-study tool for exposure to the target language. One reason that may explain why fewer encourage students to use the Web for research and reference than for self-study in the target language may be that it is considered less relevant to the curriculum. A large number of staff teach literature, which has contributed to a strong belief that material available on the Web is not particularly suited for literary study. Curiously, 36% of staff confirmed that they encourage students to use on-line dictionaries. Although this figure is not exceptionally high, it is significant because on-line dictionaries are reputed to be less reliable and comprehensive than costly paper-based or CD-ROM dictionaries, since they are often provided free of charge. The finding implies that on-line dictionaries are becoming more reliable and valuable sources of reference for language learners and hence, increasingly, staff are recommending them to their students.

When students were asked how they use the Web, 54% admitted to using the Web to research essay topics, while 45% use them to access newspapers printed in the target language and radio and television broadcasts respectively (N=82). The results from both staff and student questionnaires on this issue show that the Web is promoted as a vehicle for self-study, providing students with a range of reference and target language material. Self-study is an intrinsic part of Cambridge academic life: this may be one of the reasons why there are fewer contact hours at Cambridge dedicated to language learning and grammar than in other universities – students are expected to develop much of their linguistic competence through independent work and their year abroad.

This approach to self-study also seems to be one of the reasons why few staff use the Web as a means of delivering lecture notes or other material. It appears to be considered solely the students' responsibility to obtain that information: if they do not attend lectures, then they need to engage in further independent reading and research to catch up, rather than expecting the tutors to provide notes, in electronic format for example. Furthermore, following discussions with them, it seems that students and staff use lectures as an opportunity to evaluate ideas expressed, develop analytical skills and learn about interesting perspectives, rather than recording verbatim accounts of everything said in the lecture. Lectures tend not to take the form of historical or narrative descriptions (which can be a characteristic of area studies) and more that of tough-provoking discussions, where it is not crucial to note down every detail. Providing notes in electronic format seems, therefore, unnecessary.

MML Electronic resources: CALL packages

Although the production of Web-based material is expanding and more departments are beginning to publish on the Web, more staff and departments are involved in the creation of networked-based CALL resources. Staff from five departments have created translation exercises using *TransIT Tiger*. The texts are usually previous translation examinations, for which *TransIT Tiger* is particularly useful because it allows staff to add hints, examples of mistakes made by previous examination candidates and contextual information, in a hyperlinked format. During the 2001/02 academic year, some staff used these banks of translations in class, requiring their students to complete the translations on screen and, in some cases, asked their students to e-mail them their work.

The German department has been particularly active in the area of CALL software production, notably in the design of a self-correcting specimen examination paper for German students in Tripos Part IA and B, using the *ToolBox* authoring shell. The specimen examination tests focus on mastery of idiom and are still at the prototype stage. A more advanced and ambitious project by staff in the German department and the CALL Officer has been the design and production of *Video+*, a CD-based CALL program, published by Arnold, containing video comprehension exercises. This package is commercially available and is aimed at A-Level German students and first year undergraduates.

Whereas there is a substantial range of networked CALL programs at Cambridge, they are not used to maximum effect. 46% of student respondents (where N=82) said they use CALL programs. Since this questionnaire was administered by e-mail, the name and year group of each student was recorded and this information revealed that the largest group of respondents who confirmed they use CALL programs was first year students (21 out of the 38 respondents who admitted to using CALL). The questionnaire discovered, too, that final year students were least likely to have ever used these types of computer programs (2 out of 38 positive responses to this question were received from students in Tripos Part II). This trend implies that students in the early stages of their course of study in the MML Faculty are more likely to encounter CALL than those nearing the end of their course. This pattern is understandable given that the use of CALL at Cambridge has been evolutionary, and each year an increasing number of packages becomes available to students. It was really only in 1996 that CALL packages were adopted in earnest by the

Faculty and the range of packages available at that time and for the next two years (when the current finalists were embarking upon their course of study in MML) was more limited than nowadays. Students confirmed that the most commonly used CALL packages are those that provide grammar practice and theory, such as *GramEx* and *GramDef* (a DOS-based package, known as *Luisa* is used extensively for Italian grammar work) – 92% of the students who admitted using CALL (N=38) used these types of packages.

This further explains why the use of CALL among final year respondents to the questionnaire was more limited than among other year groups since there are fewer classes in areas like grammar for finalists. They are therefore less likely to have classes that would use CALL packages than students in first and second year who have one hour per week of classes which study areas like grammar. As a result, final year students who responded to the questionnaire were given little directed guidance in the use of CALL than students in other year groups. It is expected, however, that since students currently in years one and two are more likely to encounter CALL than their counterparts from two or three years earlier, the use of CALL among final year students will grow over time because of increased familiarity with these types of programs in the early stages of their degree courses. Nevertheless, it seems unlikely that the use of CALL among finalists will equal or exceed that of first and second years, due mainly to the lack of classes that use CALL: if final year students wish to use CALL for grammar work, for example, they are required to do so as part of their independent study time rather than being directed by tutors in classes and this raises the question of maintaining student motivation and encouraging students to find time in their Tripos Part II schedules to fit in this additional work. This evidence of poor final year usage of CALL supports Gillespie (1994: 154) and Jones (1986: 178), who believe in the importance of focusing independent learning with CALL around class work and therefore integrating it more fully into the curriculum.

When students were asked how often they used CALL programs, some patterns emerged from the results. Of the 38 respondents who confirmed that they have used CALL packages, 24% said they use packages approximately once per week, while 2.6% use them once per day. Almost half of the thirty-eight respondents (47%) said they used CALL near or during examination periods. As illustrated earlier, some CALL packages, like *TransIT Tiger*, have banks of exercises and translations and annotated exam questions from previous years, which are particularly useful for exam revision. This is obviously one of the principal reasons why a large percentage use CALL near examinations. This finding also highlights another important aspect of modern languages courses at Cambridge – they are clearly examination-orientated. Quantitative and qualitative evidence suggests that whereas networked CALL resources are used quite extensively in examination periods, this high usage is not sustained throughout the year. This may lead students to perceive that the CALL facilities there are useful solely in preparation for exams, giving them little incentive to use CALL regularly throughout the year.

Staff attitudes towards CALL seem to be similar to those of students. When asked about their use of CALL, 38% (N=42) of staff stated that they use CALL in class and 40% of them said they encourage students to use it independently, for examination revision, for example. These results suggest that a reasonable number of staff either directly use CALL for teaching purposes or exhort their students to use it in their own time. Although it might be expected that the emphasis on self-study at Cambridge and the clear orientation towards examination preparation ought to mean that a higher proportion of staff would encourage its independent use, the percentage of staff who do so is only marginally higher than the number who use it in class. Therefore, just as the popularity of a product is only as successful as its marketing strategy, the use of CALL by students is dependent on its endorsement by staff, and it can hardly be expected that vast numbers of students will use CALL unless they are exhorted to do so. There are several reasons that may help to explain why CALL is not used more by staff. One of the main reasons is its perceived value. Some staff and students remarked in their questionnaires that they feel the use of Computer-Assisted Language-Learning programs is required for successful completion of the degree courses – the curriculum does not require it. A second reason seems to be the range of resources available: one French language teaching officer remarked that, whereas he uses *GramEx* to teach grammar to his students in Tripos Part IA, he felt that the grammar topics covered by the package were very limited and provided enough material for only nine or ten hours work. A more valuable alternative for him and other tutors could be to allow them to create their own materials and design exercises. Several tutors, however, commented in both interviews and questionnaires that this would require a great deal of time – time which few of them felt they could afford given their other duties. Consequently, it is easy to see why staff seem discouraged from using CALL. Unless these problems of perception and time and resource management are dealt with, it is difficult to see how CALL can be used more extensively in MML. There is not a short-term solution to these problems. These issues, though, demonstrate the importance of developing a flexible learning and teaching culture to ensure that potential problems using computer technology can be dealt with rather than remaining insurmountable.

Language Centre resources

In addition to teaching practical language courses, the Language Centre provides a large range of electronic resources for language learners. All these resources are made available on the Language Centre's intranet that can be accessed from any computer linked to the *CUDN*, using a Web browser. Most of the resources are available to any student, meaning that students from the MML Faculty can access them. The resources provided by the Language Centre on its intranet can be divided into two categories: archived reference material and interactive activities.

The Language Centre provides two forms of reference material: off-air video recordings and listening comprehensions. The off-air recordings are digitised broadcasts of evening news bulletins, available in nine languages, including six of the MML Faculty languages (French, German, Italian, Portuguese, Russian and Spanish). These broadcasts are prepared twice or three times per week by a team of two technicians in the Language Centre who record news broadcasts on VHS tape and then convert them into three digitised formats – RealVideo and MPEG to reduce the amount of network bandwidth

126

required to watch these recordings (using the latter format, the recordings are downloaded to hard disk of the local computer, instead of being streamed across the University network) and to ensure that they can be accessed on any platform. Each digitised broadcast is available on the intranet for three-four weeks (French, German and Spanish off-air broadcasts are removed after three weeks). On occasions, the Language Centre will provide off-air recordings of feature programmes, including historical or political documentaries dealing with issues in the target language countries. Although the video quality of these off-air recordings is not yet as good as VHS, on small screen format across the high-speed network the quality is very high and the audio quality is almost perfect. Although not exactly a substitute for live broadcasts in the target language, they provide authentic exposure to the target language and, by being accessible from any networked point within the University, including colleges, students can access them in their own bedrooms or computing rooms in college at any time. This makes the off-air digitised broadcasts more flexible than VHS recordings or live broadcasts.

The Centre provides digitised listening comprehension passages for three languages on its intranet: French, German and Spanish. These comprehensions are digitised versions of previous MML Faculty listening comprehension examinations (some dating back to 1995), and transcriptions of the listening passages as well as model answers. This bank of listening comprehensions is particularly valuable for examination practice and revision, although students have year-round access to the material.

The Language Centre makes other target language material available on-line: this material normally requires the user to interact with it through a structured activity: these can be divided into two types: generic language exercises and activities relating to the Cambridge University Language Programme (CULP). Generic exercises have mainly been provided for three languages – French, German and Spanish. One of these exercises, which is used by the MML Faculty, is a grammar diagnostics test that all first year French students must complete during their first term. The test, which was introduced for the first time in October 2000 for the one hundred and fifty first year French students, takes place on-line (through the

Language Centre's intranet) and lasts forty-five minutes (the time taken to complete each test is logged by the Language Centre server). The test is marked automatically and the results are collated by Language Centre technicians and sent to the Faculty French staff who, in turn, use the results as a measure of the general level of grammar among their students.

The Centre provides a number of other self correcting tests or quizzes for French, ranging from quizzes on aspects of French geography, history and society, including a quiz based on a digitised video passage dealing with 'La Francophonie', to exercises dealing with grammar terminology and the understanding of French numbers. These exercises are mainly targeted at beginners' level students of French, although they are particularly suitable for MML students in need of remedial work in the areas of grammar and lexis. Similar interactive exercises and activities for German and Spanish are also available through the Language Centre's intranet. Language Centre staff provide most of these resources, although Faculty members, in Spanish for example, have provided video comprehension passages and exercises and Language Centre technicians have made them available on the Centre's intranet.

Unlike most other language resources available across the Language Centre intranet, some material is restricted to students enrolled in the CULP. This is a course for non-specialist language learners of French and German from across the University who have three hours of classes each week. Two hours are completed in a classroom and the third hour takes place on-line. Although students are free to choose when they complete the on-line hourly session during the week, participation in the on-line sessions is a prerequisite of successful completion of CULP. All work carried out on-line is stored on a server in the Language Centre and checked regularly by tutors. The exercises that students complete take the form of the self-correcting quizzes and listening passages, usually dealing with his-torical and cultural aspects of the target language country. There are activities for beginners and intermediate non-specialist students, however some of this material would clearly be useful for *ab initio* or first year Faculty-level students. Although still in its infancy, it is expected that the CULP course will provide more on-line material, with a view to changing the course format to one hour face-to-face teaching and two hours on-line.

Although the Web is not extensively used by MML staff to develop and publish material, it is an important part of the Cambridge Language Centre. Neither students nor staff were directly asked about these resources in their questionnaires, although some students commented that they have used them, particularly in response to the final question ('Do you consider that the computer is beneficial or disadvantageous to your language learning?'). It is difficult therefore to gauge staff and student attitudes towards these resources fully. Server statistics provided by the Language Centre, though, show that certain resources are widely used.

During the month of May 2000, the banks of archived listening examination comprehensions for French, German and Spanish were accessed over 2500 times. Whereas this figure is high, it was recorded during the examination period and students would be very keen to practice for their listening examination. Server statistics from the months of October, November and December 2000 reveal less extensive usage: the French listening comprehensions were accessed eighty-nine times in October, one hundred and nineteen in November and only nineteen times in December: the figures for German and Spanish listening comprehension were lower. This shows that the banks of listening comprehensions are really only used extensively near examination periods, confirming a similar pattern in the levels of student CALL usage.

Another resource that seems to enjoy extensive usage is the off-recordings, especially those available in French, German and Spanish. According to server figures, French off-air recordings were accessed two hundred and eighty-nine times in October; German recordings were used one hundred and sixty-nine times and the Spanish recordings were downloaded one hundred and twenty-nine times. These figures are higher than those for the listening comprehensions for the same period. Although, it is important to remember that the off-recordings are normally provided three times per week and require a team of two technicians to prepare the material each day from 9.00am to 4.00pm, making them more labour intensive than the listening comprehensions. These findings reveal an important issue about the use of electronic language-learning resources: a great deal of effort and commitment (not least financial) is required to prepare this material and although students may use the resources, their use may not reflect the effort spent in producing them. This is a widespread problem that many language resource centres and units face regularly but it illustrates the need to integrate these resources into the languages curriculum. The electronic resources prepared by the Cambridge Language Centre are primarily for self-study: students will access the banks of listening comprehensions when they want to practice for exams and view the off-air recordings to practice their aural skills but, as the server statistics show, the numbers of students accessing this material can be erratic.

The fact that two technicians are involved in preparing off-recordings each week highlights another important issue: prioritising resources. At the moment, considerable time is spent preparing off-air recordings: this means that the technicians have little time to prepare other material for MML staff, for example, such as digitised video comprehensions like those used by members of the department of Spanish and Portuguese. On the other hand, one of the reasons why so much effort is spent preparing the off-air recordings was that there had been little interest among MML staff to prepare and develop digitised material for their classes and technicians decided to employ their time fruitfully on other tasks. The Language Centre is not part of the MML Faculty and language tutors are expected to develop computer-based material with the help of the CALL Officer – this seems to explain why few Faculty members have used the Language Centre in the preparation of class material. Nevertheless, the Centre has developed considerable expertise in the production of digitised video and audio material and has a wider range of equipment and dedicated staff than the MML Faculty. A number of Faculty staff have recognised these benefits and, according to the Language Centre technicians, more MML staff are beginning to approach them, seeking their help in preparing digitised material, notably video comprehensions.

It is worth comparing the server statistics for the off-air recordings and video comprehension material, discussed above, with those of the Cambridge University Language Programme (CULP). During the months of October and November 2000, the electronic material for

French component of the CULP programme, was accessed over three thousand one hundred times and seven thousand times respectively. The CULP, of course, makes extensive use of computer technology and students are required to complete part of it on-line. This means that those enrolled in the course must access electronic resources as part of the course. The resultant server statistics clearly show that the CULP resources are more extensively used than the other Language Centre material because of their relevance to their course of study and integration into that curriculum.

Electronic resources at Cambridge are not used as widely as they might be. With few exceptions, the Web is not exploited as a medium for course delivery and attitudes towards its use show that many staff and students prefer to use the Web as a source of reference instead. The use of networked CALL and Language Centre material is variable, depending on the time of year and, at least at present, it seems that the considerable effort spent developing the material is not reflected in the level of use they receive from students and staff because of their relevance to MML courses. Nevertheless, a number of consolidated attempts are currently being made to integrate further the use of computer resources and facilities into language learning and teaching – the most obvious has been the creation of a CALL Facility.

CALL facility

In the mid 1990s, the Faculty board of MML took a major policy decision to invest in CALL. In addition to appointing a CALL Officer, the Faculty would construct a dedicated CALL Facility. This Facility would contain multimedia PCs and run an extensive platform of CALL software. In September 2000, the CALL Facility was reopened after a period of refurbishment. It is located in the Raised Faculty Building and is spread over two adjoining rooms, allowing for both classroom teaching and private study to take place at the same time. The Facility contains twenty-five PCs with multimedia capabilities to record sound, view video clips and listen to audio recordings. It is not a general purpose computing laboratory: students do not have access to printing facilities; access to generic programs like word processing software are limited and e-mail is restricted.

The Facility provides local CALL and Web language-learning resources for twelve languages: the largest selection of resources is available for French and Spanish. A number of server-based CALL programs are offered by the Facility, including pronunciation packages like *Pronunciation Tutor, Encounters* and *Cognate Language Teacher*; grammar packages such as *GramEx* and *GramDef* and translation tools like *TransIT Tiger*. Other programs, like concordances and corpora, are available for literature analysis and study. In addition, the CALL Facility provides server-based dictionaries for seven languages, including three dictionaries for French alone.

The CALL Facility maintains a number of Web pages on the MML website, providing a gateway of external Web links for all twelve languages. These links for each language are divided into categories, such as newspapers, radio and television stations and discussion lists. The website also contains a catalogue of all software available through the CALL Facility as well as a timetable of classes and induction notes for new students to the Facility.

All these internal and external resources are made available on a common desktop in the CALL Facility. This desktop contains links to other useful sources of information, including a shortcut to the MML library website and an information page, explaining how to type accents and Cyrillic characters. This common desktop is available outside the CALL Facility: the recently refurbished MML Library now has a small computer room with twelve PCs, which provides access to the CALL desktop and associated programs. In addition, the CALL Officer has set up a networking service (MML-NS), which allows MML students and staff to access the CALL desktop (and programs) from a remote computer, in a college bedroom or computing laboratory, for example. The remote computer needs to be configured to access the MML-NS and some computers, including those linked to the Public Workstation Facility (PWF), will not currently run it because they use a different login client (Novell login as opposed to Windows login). The main purpose of the MML-NS was to enable students to access CALL packages and server dictionaries from their college during the refurbishment of the CALL

Facility when services were severely disrupted. It still remains in place, giving its users the flexibility to use its resources remotely outside the CALL Facilty's opening hours (8.45am–5.30pm, Mon–Fri, during term time).

The stated aim of the CALL Facility is to integrate the use of information technology into the Faculty's teaching and learning. How is the theory applied in practice? In reality, the lab is not used as much as it could and deserves to be. Teaching time in the Facility varies from week to week, although during February 2001 for example, it was used for an average of five hours per week. One of the preferred activities for language classes in the Facility is grammar revision and practice, using packages like *GramEx*. Although, since students in Tripos IA and B receive only one hour of 'Use of French/German/ Spanish…' language classes per week, tutors prefer not to spend this hour in the CALL Facility every week, using it instead periodically as break from normal class routine.

The Facility is used for a number of other teaching activities, such as Web searching and pronunciation exercises. In these classes, the tutor plays the role of a facilitator, there to guide students and help with any problems, especially technical ones, which they may have. One new course in the MML Faculty – the Certificate in Humanities Computing for Languages, is currently the main user of the CALL Facility with three hours of classes each week in one of the CALL Facility rooms.

Students use the Facility for a number of private study activities. The lack of generic programs like MS Word and an e-mail system with a straightforward graphical user interface means that students tend not to use the lab for general tasks. Furthermore, the Facility closes at 5.30pm for security reasons and this means that students cannot use it later in the evening, when they would often have more time because they are not in class. Those who visit the Facility outside teaching time therefore tend to use it exclusively for CALL packages and other private study activities and the numbers using it will vary according to time of the year. Furthermore, the CALL Facility is located in the Raised Faculty Building, where students do not seem to congregate very often. Consequently, it is generally not used by students who are just passing by, but rather by those who make special effort to visit the computer room. Before being refurbished in 2000, the CALL Facility was located in a more central location for students in the Raised Faculty Building and would be used regularly throughout the day, particularly for e-mail access. This led to queues forming at computers and some students would spend long periods of time checking their e-mails, meaning that other students who wanted to use CALL packages were prevented from doing so. This was one of the main reasons why e-mail access in the CALL Facility was limited after the refurbishment, although it is difficult to say whether this decision has helped the CALL Facility. Whereas the rooms are now freer, which gives students more unfettered access to CALL packages, there are certainly not queues of students waiting to use the computers. One might argue that at least if students were attracted into the CALL Facility, to use e-mail, for example, or to type up or even print out essays, they would stumble across CALL packages or other similar programs and the considerable efforts made by teaching staff and the CALL Officer in the design of CALL software would be somehow rewarded.

The CALL Facility contains many valuable resources for MML students and staff but is not being used to (or even near) its full potential. The Faculty have recognised the problem of access to the CALL Facility in the evening and approved the installation of a swipe card system, which will allow students access to the CALL computer rooms outside office hours: this system has not yet been installed, however. Furthermore, the academic year 2002/03 will see the conversion of the Facility to PWF (Public Workstation Facility), which will provide students with access to a common range of generic programs and facilities, effectively converting the CALL Facility into a more general purpose computing room. When this conversion takes place, students will be able to login to their PWF accounts from other computer rooms throughout the University, including in some colleges, and access all CALL packages that have hitherto only been available in the CALL Facility, MML Library Computing room or across the MML Network Service. Conversion to PWF could lead to the CALL Facility becoming a more integral lab for language students, instead of a specialist room that they would only use (sometimes) for private study or near examination time to access

134

banks of translations and other past papers. Paradoxically however, since students will be able to access the CALL material from other locations across the University, this may discourage students from using the CALL Facility who, instead, will use PWF rooms nearer to their college, for example.

In another important development, the computers in the CALL Facility will be linked to a live satellite feed, allowing students to watch live target language television from the computers. Students would normally visit the Language Centre (hitherto located at the Sidgwick site, near the MML Raised Faculty Building and CALL Facilty) to watch live satellite broadcasts. However during the 2001/02 academic year, the Centre made the decision to move off the Sidgwick site to a more central location in the city. Since many languages students have classes on the Sidgwick site of the University, students may prefer to watch satellite broadcasts there instead of walking or cycling to the new Language Centre site. Consequently, the addition of live satellite television in the CALL Facility could draw more students to it, possibly even students who only have used the Language Centre resources in the past. This could be one way of encouraging students to make a natural association between computers and language learning: a view advocated by Ross (1991: 66). She believes that, in order to ensure computer technology brings maximum benefit to the language learner, it is important for students to feel that computer work is as important and integral to their language as watching target language videos and similar activities.

This development strongly suggests that the MML Faculty has recognised the need to move away from a specially dedicated languages computing lab to a more general one, offering a wider range of facilities to their students. This decision could ensure that the CALL Facility (or whatever name it may subsequently take) becomes a more central part of the language teaching and learning experience for students and staff in the MML Faculty.

Learning approaches

The use of computer technology in Cambridge allows for a more constructivist approach to learning, through the availability and use of banks of self-study CALL material. The use of technology for behaviourist learning is more limited, with few teacher-centred classes making extensive use of the technology. The limited opportunity for computer-mediated behaviourist learning seems to explain why computer technology is not always used in the teaching process.

Planning a computer-based language-learning environment

Computer technology is used quite extensively in learning and teaching at Cambridge but this does not mean that the institution intended to create a computer-based language-learning environment. The extent to which the environment has been strategically planned can be seen in the role of management in establishing computer technology at the centre of the learning and teaching process

Role of management: training

If the wide range of computer resources available to staff and students is to be properly used, it is obvious that both groups need to be trained in their use and feel comfortable with the facilities; otherwise there is a danger that the technology will be perceived as a complicated obstacle to their learning and teaching. At Cambridge, there are two main types of computer training available to staff and students: faculty-wide and UCS induction. In addition, since many colleges have different standards of computing facilities – some more complex than others – some college computing officers will provide induction for their students; not surprisingly, though, the level of this form of induction varies from college to college.

Each year, the University Computing Service arranges an IT training course for all University staff and students. The course provides induction in general areas, such as the use of the Web, e-mail and word processing applications, as well as more complex areas like programming, in addition to desktop publishing. Although these courses are available to everyone at Cambridge, UCS staff have noticed that most of the taught courses are attended by postgraduates and teaching staff rather than undergraduates. This confirms the findings of the previous case study, where many undergraduates already feel very competent using computers, without undergoing a training course. In light of the poor undergraduate attendance on these courses, the Computing Service are currently reviewing their induction process and are also considering the introduction of the widely recognised European Computer Driving Licence (ECDL) to encourage a larger proportion of undergraduate students to undergo formal induction in the use of the computer.

Whereas the UCS offers one form of induction – usually providing general computer training – more detailed training in the specialised computer facilities offered by MML Faculty is important. While students may consider themselves to be proficient in the use of e-mail or Web surfing and staff use e-mail regularly for administration, neither group will necessarily understand how the computer can be effectively used for language learning and teaching. Recognising this, as well as the envisaging the possibility that students and staff will not use the extensive electronic language learning-resources available to them, the CALL Officer provides training for staff and students.

All MML students receive induction in the use of the computer for language learning. This induction normally takes the form of an introductory one-hour lecture, during the first week of term in October (the notes from which are made available on-line for the rest of the year). Obviously, one lecture is inadequate to provide a thorough induction and it is designed as a taster, with other courses being offered during the year in the CALL Facility, to provide more in-depth training. These courses are, however, not scheduled regularly (one or twice a term, sometimes less), due, in part, to the considerable time constraints on staff, like the CALL Officer, who arrange such sessions.

In order to provide more systematic induction at Faculty level and to encourage students to make full use of the computer for language learning purposes, the 2000/2001 academic year saw the introduction of a pilot computing certificate that became a fully validated course at Cambridge in the 2001/02 academic year. The CALL Officer, along with colleagues from the department of Spanish and Portuguese, delivers this course, called the 'Certificate in Humanities Computing for Languages' (CHUCOL). This year-long course is taught for three hours each week in the CALL Facility (normally one hour of lectures and two hours of practical work). It begins with some basic computer training and then moves towards more complex areas like Web page design and the use of digital audio and video material, as well as the theory and practice of CALL. Lecture notes, in outline form, in addition to a weekly schedule of classes and assignment details, are available on the CHUCOL website.[1] The course is based entirely on coursework and all students must complete a project on any CALL or Humanities computing field, creating a basic CALL program, for example, in addition to designing websites in the target language and critically evaluating software or external websites. This course has quite an advanced content and workload: upon successful completion of it, though, students will be awarded an academically validated certificate. The course, however, currently only has a maximum of twenty places and it does not seem likely that this number will increase significantly because of funding considerations. Therefore, only a tiny percentage of the faculty undergraduates have the opportunity to complete this computer course and, although the development of the CHUCOL is an indication of the Faculty's determination to provide a systematic induction course for language students, it does not address the computing needs or train all the MML students in the use of the computer for language learning purposes.

One of the major difficulties in providing staff training is the problem of arranging sessions during the academic year at times suitable for staff to attend. This is due to the very substantial workload

1   See http://www.mml.cam.ac.uk/call/cert/ Accessed on the WWW, April 2001.

of colleagues and, since most of them are spread across the city (some only teach in their colleges), this makes it more difficult to arrange training sessions. Often, therefore, it is unproductive to arrange any kind of training for staff during term time because these sessions would almost certainly be poorly attended. This is one of the reasons why staff training in the MML Faculty is more irregular than student training. Such training normally takes the form of one-off seminars, demonstrating the resources available in the CALL Facility. Other sessions have been arranged, dealing with specific issues like sending and receiving attachments on e-mail and Web publication. At the end of the Christmas term in 2000/01, language tutors who teach 'Use of French' courses held a seminar in the CALL Facility to look at ways of integrating the computer further into their teaching. The workshop has led to two members of the French department developing a textual comprehension activity, involving the use of the Web and e-mail. It also proposed the development of a bank of supplementary translations on *TransIT Tiger* for student private study.

Staff training in the use of the computing for language teaching and learning is therefore erratic, although it appears very impractical to provide a more systematic training programme: it has been suggested that the CHUCOL course for students be offered to staff also, however time constraints during term time may make this unworkable and it might be scheduled for the summer months.

Computer training offered to students and staff is therefore variable and this reflects the varying levels of computer literacy between both groups. Systematic training in the use of computer technology for language learning, though remains crucial: 67% of staff and 51% of students felt inadequately trained in this area. Faculty provision of suitable training is quite limited, mainly due to constraints on time and human resources. The Faculty is committed to changing this situation, although there does seem to be a globally suitable solution. Training, though, is not the only way of integrating the computer into language learning and teaching and therefore into establishing it as a central part of the learning environment: another way of doing so is by making the computer a central part of everyday life for students and staff at Cambridge.

The computer potentially seems to have an important role in everyday University life. Although e-mail has become an important tool for ensuring fast and efficient communication within the University, another way that information is disseminated electronically is through the University newspaper. Published every week, *The University Reporter* (often shortened to *The Reporter*) is the official University newspaper. All University reports, announcements, details of University business and appointments are published in it. At the start of each academic year, lecture lists are printed in *The Reporter*, giving times and venues for each lecture, listed by faculty. Towards the end of term, examination timetables are published in the newspaper and, after the examination period, the official results and class lists appear in it. It is available in hard copy throughout the University and since 1997 has been available on-line through the University's website. Each edition is archived and can easily be searched on-line: this allows students to look up previous year's examination results or any other information from previous and contemporary editions. By publishing such important information as examination results and timetables, students and staff are almost compelled to consult it regularly and, for many, the most flexible way of doing so is by using the on-line edition. This, in turn, encourages students and staff to use the Web regularly. By encouraging them to do so, this further promotes the concept of an electronic communications culture within the institution. It also encourages users to make a more natural association between computer technology and its application to other aspects of everyday university life, such as teaching and learning.

The University has one of the largest libraries in the United Kingdom (it is one of the five British Copyright Libraries), with almost seven million volumes in its main University Library (UL). Given the dispersed nature of Cambridge, it is no surprise that there are several libraries throughout the University, including the MML Faculty Library, and a library in each college. Cambridge libraries offer a number of electronic facilities to students and staff: these include electronic catalogues and some electronic resources, like journals. The quality of computer facilities in each of the libraries varies across the colleges and faculties. At the moment, all libraries do not operate a fully electronic catalogue. The main UL is a good example of this. With such a vast collection of books, the process of cataloguing all of them is a mammoth task and the paper catalogue system is still used for most of the UL material. In several cases, the entries are handwritten. Most college and faculty libraries (though not all of them) use a common electronic Web-based and Telnet catalogue, but it does not offer staff and students a complete database of all books and material in all the libraries. Equally, the catalogue can only be used to check the availability of books and other material: it cannot be used to make reservations, renew loans or provide any other borrower information. Students in the UL must use one of several dedicated Telnet catalogue terminals to access borrower information; they cannot, however, make reservations.

In other Cambridge libraries, like the MML Library, students must ask a member of the library staff to access their borrower information. This system seems quite outdated considering that access to borrower information through electronic catalogues has existed in many universities for at least ten years, although one of the main reasons for limiting access to borrower information is to ensure that books and other materials are closely monitored. If a student wishes to renew a loan, he must return the book to the issue desk, thereby showing that he has not lost it, instead of renewing the loan on-line: given the vast numbers of books in the University libraries, it is obviously important to ensure close monitoring of them. The libraries though offer an electronic borrower notification system, called EMICS. If students register for this service, automated messages will be sent to their e-mail accounts to remind them when to return books. E-mails are sent out a minimum of two days in advance of the deadlines; books can also be recalled and students and staff can be notified when requested books become available. Although students and staff are not compelled to register for this service, it encourages those who have registered to check their e-mail regularly and makes electronic mail more important and central to everyday life at the University.

There is a substantial range of electronic resources available through the University of Cambridge Libraries' website. These include an indexed list of electronic journals, some of which are openly available through external websites or require a password; others are CD-ROM based and can only be accessed from computers connected to the *CUDN*. Their extent of material for language students, though, is more limited. The Libraries' website, however, provides access to resources indexed by language: these mainly take the form of citation and bibliographical indexes and occasionally electronic books and periodicals. Students, of course, have flexible access to many of these resources, accessing them from their college bedroom or computer room.

The computer plays a significant role in some key everyday activities at Cambridge, although the electronic resources in the University Libraries are less advanced than might be expected in such a prestigious institution. It is possible, of course, for students and staff to avoid using computer technology in these areas and, as a result, it appears that its use is not as central to the University environment as it could be.

Management support

Senior management at central and faculty level play other important roles in planning a computer-based environment. One of these is providing a financial infrastructure to support the development of technology. The MML Faculty is, according to a number of senior faculty administrators, one of the most technologically advanced in Cambridge, citing MML's widespread adoption of e-mail for communication as evidence. The Faculty is obviously well equipped with technology and staff and students have access to powerful computer hardware and software. This observation is supported by the results from staff and student questionnaires. When questioned about the quality of the Faculty's computer equipment, 91% of students (N=82) and 62% of staff (N=42) said they felt the facilities were adequate. The excellent provision of computer equipment is, however, a source of contention within the Faculty. In their questionnaires and interviews, staff alluded to the University's policy of providing a wealth of funding for equipment but being unwilling to fund additional support

142

staff (such as technicians) to maintain these facilities. The MML Faculty, for example, was only given permission to appoint its first permanent full-time computer technician at the end of the 2000/01 academic year.

Whereas the Faculty was given permission to appoint a CALL Officer in 1996, it appears evident that one full-time appointment to this post does not seem to be sufficient to cope with all the duties and responsibilities of the position. The demands of continually updating and adding CALL software and assisting staff with the development of courseware and other electronic resources are considerable. The increasing demands on the CALL Officer and the fact that increasing numbers of tutors are approaching him for advice on developing their own electronic materials are encouraging signs for they show that interest in using computer technology is growing among staff. On the other hand, though, if the CALL Officer is unable to respond to all these demands and deal with requests from staff immediately because of other pressing demands, staff could become frustrated and decide to postpone their projects for courseware development or even abandon them altogether. There are signs of improvement to this situation. The newly-appointed computer technician for MML has now taken over the responsibility of maintaining the Faculty website from the CALL Officer, thereby giving the CALL Officer more time to devote to his other duties.

A major obstacle to the integration of computer technology in the Faculty is the problem of demotivation. Several members of staff who are interested in using ICT further in their teaching remarked that they do not feel they have the time to explore its possibilities because the University does not give them enough time to attend training sessions or develop courseware. This raises another major issue: the importance that the University attributes to developing computer-based learning and teaching. If staff are expected to develop electronic resources and learn how to use the technology in their own time, as opposed to using sabbaticals for this purpose, many tutors will be simply unable to find time to do so. Furthermore, it sends out a clear message to staff: the development of electronic courseware are not viewed important enough work to merit study leave, but rather it seems to be considered as a hobby or sideline for the staff concerned.

This has also led to the perception that any research articles produced as a result of the development and use of electronic courseware is not considered as academically important as other areas of research that have a long standing tradition, such as literature. This has ramifications for staff, perhaps when applying for promotion. Evidence of this attitude can be found at lower levels of management, such as heads of departments. In the 2000/01 academic year, the head of a department in MML requested the transfer of one of his staff from a CALL project to another project that was considered more important: the CALL project has been subsequently suspended. King *et al.* (1998: 15) argue that if computer technology is to be integrated into learning and teaching, management need to be sympathetic to and supportive of staff involved in courseware development and similar initiatives. If staff perceive there to be very few rewards to their efforts in developing electronic resources and courseware, it is more than likely that only those who have a true passion for this type of work will continue, whilst others may feel that the disadvantages (such as the time and work required) outweigh the benefits.

The use of ICT in MML and the development of electronic resources is relatively unsystematic. The Faculty does not have a clear strategy on the use of ICT in language learning and teaching, other than the creation of a CALL Facility and appointment of a CALL Officer. There is no obvious impetus within the Faculty to develop the use of ICT and it has been left to interested members of staff to design their own electronic materials and use these in their classes. Their efforts have spurred other members of staff to do the same. The implementation of an ICT policy is bottom-up rather than top-down. The main role of senior management within the Faculty in the implementation of a potential ICT policy is to provide suitable hardware and software for staff and students. The Chairman of the Faculty Board is a rotating position and, every three years, a new chairman is appointed: each new chair will have different views on the importance of ICT in language learning and, as a result, there is little opportunity to introduce any significant ICT policy or strategy and see it implemented.

Acceptance of the value of computer technology by learners and teachers is essential if it is to become central to the process of language teaching and learning. Overall, staff considered the use of ICT as a positive and advantageous step in helping students to learn. Some cited the rapid access to information (including target language material) that is available through the World Wide Web, while others considered the effect of the novelty value of computers on students. Another common observation was the need to ensure that ICT does not replace the teacher but rather that the teacher guides students to use this technology effectively. In other words, staff feel that ICT is a pedagogical aid, there to support the teacher. They see, however that its arrival means a redefining of the teacher's role in the learning process, involving both teacher and student-centred learning, confirming the views expressed in Chapter 1. Around half of the staff respondents (48%) felt that the use of ICT encouraged students to engage in independent study, through the use of CALL programs and the Web, and only 2% felt that the use of ICT had a negative effect of their level of independent study. Equally, a limited number of staff respondents (19%) felt that students wanted a reduction in the use of ICT in language and literature classes. The generally positive attitude of staff, though, shows that they see the benefits for using ICT in learning and teaching, and therefore support its use in principle, although this enthusiasm is not as evident in practice.

In general, the attitude of students was enthusiastic. Many students considered ready access to target language material on the Web (such as on-line broadcasts and target language newspapers) as a major advantage and the Language Centre off-air recordings were seen as particularly valuable. In addition, many respondents felt that CALL packages dealing with grammatical understanding were useful. On the other hand, students felt generally uneasy with the notion that the computer might be used as language teachers. Some students echoed the opinion expressed by staff that ICT is not a replacement for the human tutor. This indicates that students feel the computer is beneficial for certain areas of language learning and that they recognise the limitations of computer technology, in particular the coherency of Web, which supports Haworth (1996: 180). The concern about computers turning into teachers seems to demonstrate a degree of misunderstanding about the concept of computer-based language learning. This term does not mean tutor replacement, it means tutor and learner enhancement, through the use of computer technology. The fact that students do not always understand that suggests that one of the main barriers to the creation of computer-based learning environment is how to convince people that it is does not intend to lead to the depersonalisation of the classroom and the onset of staff redundancies!

The overall attitude expressed by staff and students in MML was positive and shows that many of them believe the computer has an important impact on learning and teaching, which implies that they see the benefits of using computers as an integral part of the language learning and teaching experience in the University. The evidence of staff usage of ICT in their current pedagogy, though, suggests that there are some obstacles that prevent the increasing integration of computer technology into language learning and teaching from becoming a reality in this University. One of these is curriculum relevance.

Curriculum relevance

A number of aspects of modern languages degree courses at Cambridge make it very difficult to achieve maximal integration of the computer into the learning and teaching environment for students and staff. Some of these have already been discussed, including the preference for handwritten work that has led some members of staff to discourage their students from submitting work in word-processed or electronic format.

One aspect that many staff made reference to in their questionnaires and interviews is the perception that the use of the computer and, in particular, CALL packages, is only useful for language acquisition *per se* and not relevant in the broader MML curriculum. One tutor remarked in his questionnaire response that 'the curriculum/ course [at Cambridge] is not particularly suited, or one could say, it does not require ICT to complete it successfully'. Students expressed a similar view during discussions with them and one made the following comment in his questionnaire: 'the course here [Cambridge] contains so little language work that I have to spend my time on other aspects of the course for which computers are not helpful (i.e. literature/history)'. MML courses are changing and incorporating more language content each year, meaning that this issue will become less relevant as a barrier towards integrating computer technology more into learning and teaching. At the moment, however, perceived curriculum relevance appears to be a major factor in explaining why such resources as the CALL Facility are underused. This supports Oblinger (1996: 34), who discusses the view that the current teaching culture, which does not reward approaches using technology can inhibit changes to the student learning culture. In other words, if students do not see the value in using technology on their course, they seem unwilling to embrace it. It also supports Gillespie and McKee's argument that students must be able to see good reasons for using computer technology. (1999a: 41) To say, however, that the CALL Facility provides resources solely for the study of language is not true. Several resources, such as server based dictionaries and corpora that are available in the CALL Facility are particularly useful for literary analysis and the study of linguistics. Some tutors (in Spanish and Russian for example) use computer technology for more than simply language acquisition (publishing lecture notes on the Web that deal with literary themes). These initiatives are obviously useful in changing the perception of the value of computers in MML courses at Cambridge, however they are in a minority.

Another important aspect of MML courses is the heavy focus on examinations and little weighting given to coursework. Some staff have experienced problems encouraging students to complete the work they set as part of computer-based projects, such as the digitised video comprehension series for Spanish, because students do not receive any kind of continuous assessment mark that will count towards the overall mark for that paper. This means that students are being asked to do work merely for practice, and whereas some students will be willing to do this, others feel that they have too many other tasks to carry out and may only complete this work if they have some spare time. This is particularly problematic when trying to integrate computer technology into everyday learning and teaching aspects of language courses because some students will find the prospect of using computers quite daunting and discouraging. If they feel there is no kind of incentive to do so, such as a coursework mark, they may simply not do the work. The issue of introducing continuous assessment is currently being reviewed at Cambridge and one tutor has already experimented with the possibility of replacing an end of year Spanish paper with a dossier of two large essays or projects. Perhaps by removing the ostensible focus on examinations, tutors will have greater flexibility to introduce more elements to their courses that will require students to use computers and integrate these more effectively into the languages curriculum in MML.

Chapter Five
Example 3: the University of Toronto

Background information

Chosen to represent an international benchmark in this comparative study, the University of Toronto (or U of T, as it is commonly known) is the largest university in Canada.

History

With over fifty thousand full-time and part-time students, the University has three campuses, with the main campus at St George in downtown Toronto, established in the 1820s, and two smaller campuses at Mississauga (known as Erindale College), and at Scarborough, both of which are based around twenty miles from the downtown campus and were established in the 1960s. Each of the campuses enjoys a large proportion of autonomy in affairs such as accommodation, computing services, library facilities and general budgetary matters.

The institution is modelled on Cambridge University: there are six University colleges. Until recently, the colleges had a similar role to their Cambridge counterparts and they employed their own teaching staff. In 1975, in an effort to centralise teaching, colleges lost most of their teaching responsibility, with the creation of several University departments (including French and German). Some of their main functions nowadays are to provide accommodation for students, teaching rooms and office space. Colleges offer students a range of social, sports and library facilities and all students are enrolled in them when they start their programme of studies at the University. Unlike Cambridge, however, the University colleges provide very limited accommodation space.

Modern Languages are taught on all three campuses, although some staff from the St George campus teach on the Mississauga campus. Language provision on the Scarborough campus has traditionally been separate from that provided on the other two campuses, partly because languages staff on the Scarborough campus generally do not teach on the other two campuses. This made it difficult to obtain information about language learning and teaching on the Scarborough campus and, as a result, this study focuses on the language departments of the St George and Erindale campuses. There are seven languages departments and, on the St George campus alone, there are over five thousand language students. Each department belongs to the Faculty of Arts and Science, although they are each independent, both financially and administratively, of one another. French is the largest department, with over one thousand two hundred students on the St George campus, and also has a very strong role in the University, due in no small part to the bilingual nature of Canada. Staff in that department are widely dispersed across the city, many having offices in different college buildings. This problem is more acute in French than in the other languages departments because of its size, with over forty full-time faculty staff, in comparison to fifteen in the department of Spanish and Portuguese, for example.

Students too are dispersed across the city. This is partly due to their accommodation arrangements. So few students live in college accommodation (there are only places for three thousand nine hundred students in the colleges) and, as a result, students will live in privately rented accommodation in the city or commute from home. High tuition fees and a higher cost of living in Toronto in comparison to other areas in Ontario and elsewhere in Canada make it almost essential for students to hold down at least one part-time job while studying, and encourage many to commute from home to University on the outskirts of the city, in an effort to keep costs down. As a result, the sense of community that is very prevalent in Cambridge is not present in Toronto. Many students simply do not have the time to get involved in college or extra curricular social activities because of their employment commitments. Further evidence of this is the fact that students appear to have little or no affiliation or allegiance to their department – as in Cambridge – although the main difference between the two institutions is that students in Cambridge are usually well integrated into their college, helped by the small group supervision sessions with college teaching officers. In Toronto, that would be impractical because of the vast numbers of students taking courses: in one first year French module there are over one hundred and sixty students and nine instructors. Consequently, the relationship between departmental staff and students is quite distant. Students only sporadically pass through Odette Hall, which houses the French departmental offices, for example, if they are handing in work to the few French instructors based in the building or wish to speak to the secretarial staff about an administrative query. There are no noticeboards for students in Odette Hall because very few students are ever around the building to read them. In other words, there is little sign of a common social area, such as the médiathèque at Ulster.

Language courses

The vast numbers of students enrolled in Modern Languages courses paint an inaccurate picture of the nature of Modern Languages degrees at the U of T. A large proportion of students are studying language modules as part of another degree. The first year French module mentioned above is a good example (FSL161Y – Practical French). This course is a non-specialist language course for students from other faculties. Of course, many universities offer non-specialist language courses, but such courses in French are particularly attractive and highly subscribed in Canada since many businesses need staff with a working knowledge of French. The wide variety of non-specialist language courses at Toronto means that many students pick and mix language modules, only taking one or two modules in the language and then, certainly by final year, abandoning their language studies to concentrate on their main area of study. Of the one hundred and sixty students in the above first year French programme, under one third will end up specialising in French or choosing it as their major subject. In addition to these types of courses, there is a variety of specialist language degree programmes, ranging from literature and cultural studies to translation and phonetics.

Computer infrastructure

The computer infrastructure in such a large institution as Toronto is very complex.

Computer provision and management

Being based on three separate campuses, it is difficult to talk about a common computer infrastructure in the University. Until the mid-1990s, on the St George campus, there were faculty-based computer services that looked after the computing needs of the departments within their faculty, the Centre for Computing in the Humanities, for example. Just over ten years ago, the University realised that it needed to provide a more centralised approach to computing and decided to create a common infrastructure. This common infrastructure is still being implemented today, controlled by two levels of computer services: UTC (University of Toronto Computing service), which is responsible for general computing policy and provision of generic computing labs within the University, and the faculty-specific computing services. UTC is divided into local Computing Services on each campus, the largest of which is known as Information Commons, which is based on the St George campus. In the Faculty of Arts and Science, which is the largest faculty of the University, with over twenty-five thousand students, the Computing in the Arts and Social Sciences service (CHASS) provides faculty-level computing services. CHASS has responsibility for hardware and software provision and technical support for faculty staff and computer labs, including a number of multimedia labs. CHASS still has considerable respon- sibility for the computing needs of the Faculty and employs six full-time technicians, who maintain over one hundred PCs in the Faculty computing labs.

E-mail provision

Allocation of staff and student e-mail addresses in Toronto is less systematic than in the other institutions studied. Staff, on the St George campus, for example, have generally either received an account from the main University e-mail system (*UTORmail*) or from faculty Computer Services, notably CHASS. Faculty e-mail accounts, though, are now being phased out in an effort to create a common e-mail allocation system through *UTORmail* and to simplify the process of creating e-mail distribution lists. Students on all three campuses are automatically registered for e-mail when they register for their library cards. They are issued with PIN numbers that enable them to register their *UTORmail* accounts on-line and to choose their own e-mail addresses. One of the drawbacks with this type of allocation system is that that e-mail lists cannot be centrally created before the beginning of the academic year and then distributed to faculties or departments. Lists can only be created when users register for *UTORmail*, which may be several weeks after the term has started. One of the main advantages with the *UTORmail* system is that all students and staff will eventually use the same e-mail system and therefore make it easier to search e-mail directory lists. However, unless students register their *UTORmail* addresses before the beginning of the academic year or they are automatically generated for students, it is difficult to envisage the kind of centrally produced e-mail lists, available to faculties at the beginning of the year, that exist at Cambridge. The nearest equivalents to centrally provided e-mail distribution lists at Toronto are exploded distribution lists, such as those created by CHASS, for different departments. CHASS collects the e-mail addresses of staff or students as appropriate and then creates a listserv. These lists, of course, can only be created after the academic year has started, at which point interested Faculty staff can easily create their own lists, if they wish. When they register for *UTORmail*, all students are also allocated 50Mb of file storage space in their own personal Web storage area, a system know as *UTORweb*. This allows students to access files from anywhere in the world and eliminates the need to use floppy disks. By providing a common platform for file management, *UTORweb* reduces the problem of fragile storage space, which has contributed to student resistance towards using ICT (Gillespie and McKee 1999a: 40).

Networking infrastructure

The *UTORnet* – the University of Toronto's high-speed network backbone is available on all three campuses. From October 2001, the University began using wireless networking portals in all its buildings. This encourages students to use their own laptops to connect to the University network, giving them access to electronic resources. CHASS has begun looking at several proposals to establish a bank of laptop computers that students would be able to hire or borrow from the libraries. Students would then be able to connect to wireless network to surf the Web or send e-mail and submit work electronically. Each college residence is connected to the *UTORnet* and some of the residences provide their own computer rooms that are linked to the network. All bedrooms in the residences have Ethernet connections to the *UTORnet*, allowing students with their own PCs to use the University's network. However, since most students live outside residences, usually in rented accommodation, the Ethernet connections in the college dorms are of little value to them. Recognising this problem, the computing services on all three campuses have set up a large modem dial-up pool for staff and students, called *UTORdial*. At the moment, there are over twenty thousand dial-up accounts for staff and students on the St George campus alone. Users pay a minimal fee (CAN$7 for twenty hours dial-up time) and this gives students and staff access to e-mail and Web browsing facilities at a standard modem speed. University staff and students do not necessarily need to use these dial-up facilities because Internet calls throughout North America are much cheaper than in the UK, often free. For users who are interested in a higher connection speed, Computer Services have negotiated a deal with Bell Telecom (the major telecommunications

154

provider in Canada) to provide cable modems to University users at a reduced rate of $30 per month. Cable modems, in addition to providing a high connection speed (around half the speed of the *UTORnet*, and considerably faster than a standard modem), also enable remote users to use a University IP address and this allows them to access files or information (from a CD-ROM, for example) that is restricted to registered computers on the University network. Even without accessing the *UTORnet*, students have access to their files across the Web, which are saved in their *UTORweb* storage space. All this means that students and staff have almost as good access to networking facilities off-campus or at home as they have in their University office or computing lab.

Toronto, therefore, has a high-quality computing infrastructure, which is one of the basic components of a successful computer-based language-learning environment.

Computer-based language-learning in action

The computer is used in language learning and teaching in a number of main areas. Findings have been drawn from observational analysis; results from questionnaires distributed to staff and students in three modern languages departments, as well as interviews with students and staff. Questionnaires were received from sixty-four students and thirteen members of staff. Staff questionnaires were administered electronically and on paper, while student questionnaires were administered only on paper during focus group sessions with students from all four years of study, the majority of whom were taking French, on the two campuses of Mississauga and St George. Interviews were conducted with nine members of staff from the French department during two departmental meetings.

The University of Toronto in general has quite an unsystematic approach to e-mail; this has led a number of departments to use the Web in preference to e-mail clients as a means of facilitating communication between staff and students. The departments of French, German, Italian and Spanish and Portuguese have websites and they provide links to a series of course sites for each of these languages, some of which are merely on-line module descriptions but others are much more interactive. There are links to four such websites in Spanish, two in German and over twenty in French (between the two campuses of St George and Mississauga).

The interactive websites serve as a means of communication between staff and students. Many French tutors publish timetables for classes, including a schedule of lecture topics to be covered each week and contact details for instructors, as well as course resources. A few tutors use the course websites to publish information about forthcoming social events – details of films to be screened at the University cinema, information about the French Society and possibly even photographs from previous social events.

Within the French department, there is only one e-mail distribution list and it is used exclusively for staff, graduate students and teaching assistants. Until recently, announcements such as details of public lectures and social events (including the French cinema society) were sent via this e-mail distribution list to staff, who were asked to announce the information in their classes. Staff, of course, did not always pass on messages, thinking perhaps that other staff had already passed on the information in other classes and that there was little point repeating it.

This approach to communication was obviously not the most effective and it has led a number of staff to create bulletin board forums, using *NetForum*, on their course websites. One of the best examples of this is the Practical French course (FSL161 and its second year counterpart, FSL261Y), taught across the two campuses of St George and Mississauga. The bulletin board is used extensively in this course: some of the nine instructors use it to pass on information about social events, although students mainly use the board as a means of submitting their coursework to staff. The bulletin board has been designed to allow students to send messages directly to their instructors' e-mail accounts. By opting to use a Web-based bulletin board system, the designers of the course have ensured that all students use the same common system to send messages and work, giving them the same editing and formatting capabilities that can sometimes be lost when using different e-mail systems.

Other French courses use a bulletin board on their websites as a discussion forum. Sometimes participation in these on-line discussions is compulsory and participation coursework marks are awarded for it. One instructor in the German department uses a bulletin board as a help line discussion forum: students e-mail questions about the German course to him – grammar points that they do not understand, for example – and the answers to the queries are posted on the bulletin board for everyone to access.

Through the use of bulletin boards and announcement sections on course websites, the departments are trying to link students who are geographically dispersed across Toronto in an electronic environment. In the 2000/01 academic year, the French department at St George proposed to create a general bulletin board discussion forum on the department's main website for the St George campus – a system already in existence within the French department at Erindale. One of the main reasons for creating this forum was to give students a feeling of community within the department and enable them to communicate with students from other years, whom they would never meet otherwise.

Since students and staff are based in various locations across the city, communication between them can be problematic. Staff have recognised that e-mail is efficient and a fast way of communicating. Evidence of this can be found in the results of the staff questionnaire: 77% of respondents (where N=13) confirmed that they use e-mail on a regular basis for University-related tasks. 85% use it to communicate with students, while 92% correspond with colleagues by e-mail. An equally substantial percentage of respondents (85%) stated that they use e-mail to send and receive administrative documentation, such as minutes of meetings, timetable proposals and examination questions to secretarial staff. A smaller percentage use e-mail to send coursework details and receive assignments from students: 38% use e-mail to receive coursework, while 31% send work to students this way. The questionnaire revealed evidence of an e-mail culture among staff in Toronto – 92% of respondents admitted using e-mail regularly for personal activities such as contacting friends and family. These findings show that e-mail is used more for teaching support purposes and for personal use than as part of the mainstream teaching process. One reason that could explain this is that e-mail is not considered the most effective way of communicating with vast numbers of students, which is essential if passing on assignment details, for example. The lack of e-mail distribution lists also explains why bulletin boards and course websites are used regularly for communicating with large groups of students. According to the survey, 62% of staff use the Web to communicate with their students, including posting course notes, coursework details and other class information on their websites. On the other hand, however, e-mail is seen as an effective method for communicating with individual students or colleagues. These trends support the findings of Chapter 3, which discovered that staff will embrace communications technology when it is made as invisible as possible and they are not burdened with complex setup procedures.

Results from the student questionnaire show that they use e-mail less than staff. 59% (where N=64) use e-mail for University-related activities, while 86% use it for personal tasks. These results show a disparity between their use of e-mail for University tasks and their personal use of it, which seems strange among a generation of students who have grown up with electronic communication throughout school. It also seems unusual that the level of student e-mail usage is below that of staff: this appears to contradict a widely held view among academic staff that students are always streets ahead of them in using computing technology. The gulf in both areas may be explained by the fact that increasingly students do not need to use e-mail to receive information about classes and coursework – most of this can now be accessed on course websites. Furthermore 44% of students use the Web to communicate with staff, through bulletin boards, for example. This is slightly lower than their use of e-mail for communicating with staff (56%), suggesting that e-mail is marginally preferred to personal student-staff communication, although the Web

158

is catching up very quickly. The increase in popularity of the Web can be attributed to its convenience: students need to consult course websites anyway to obtain coursework and other information, so it is convenient for them to use these websites for communicating with their tutors.

Another reason that could help explain the gulf between staff and student usage is their differing levels of access to e-mail and the Web, both on and off campus. Students have access to a large pool of computers and, by extension, access to the Internet. The Robarts Library on the St George campus has over two hundred PCs, for example. Nevertheless, given the vast numbers of students across the University, there are often queues for computers in Robarts and other computing facilities and students cannot afford to spend long periods of time queuing to use them. This contrasts with the staff situation, where each colleague has his own PC in University. In addition, staff have more favourable access to the Internet from home than students: 92% of staff (N=13) and 78% of students (N=64) can access the Web and their e-mail accounts from home.

According to the views of staff and students at Toronto, there is clearly a move towards the use of the Web as a means of mass communication, while e-mail seems best suited for individual contact. Reaction to the use of e-mail may change, however with the arrival of a webmail system. As they become increasingly familiar with the more user-friendly and easily accessible webmail system, both staff and students may opt to communicate through e-mail rather than through bulletin boards and course websites, not least because it provides a more secure environment to transmit material and infor-mation (many course websites and bulletin boards at Toronto are openly available to the general public). At present, however, it is difficult to envisage this change. Until staff feel comfortable using e-mail for group communication, the Web will probably continue to be the way of communicating within the language-learning environment at Toronto.

Although used for general communication between staff and students, course websites are more often used as a bank of resources for students. The department of French website, for example, offers a gateway to French language-learning resources, including on-line grammar exercises and dictionaries. Nevertheless, some course websites, in particular, offer a very comprehensive bank of such resources: FSL161Y and FSL261Y (Practical French) are examples. In those course websites, staff have added a wide range of links for students to use when doing coursework. These links include on-line dictionaries, information about French music and composers and other cultural information that is relevant to the topics studied in class. Other material includes links to on-line radio and television stations, grammar notes, self-correcting grammar exercises, links to French libraries, revision tips for forthcoming tests. The sites also provide questions relating to topics covered in class that students will answer and submit to their instructors electronically via a bulletin board. Some staff use this audio and textual material as the basis for class activities, while other tutors ask students to use this material and complete the work in their own time. This has led to what Stepp-Greany (2002: 167), quoting Kern, describes as a role change for the teacher, which involves providing a 'scaffold for their students' learning'. In other words, the teacher directs students towards information (in this case, by providing links on the course websites). The teacher is likened to a facilitator of information, guiding students towards relevant material on the Web for use in class and also in self-study periods. This change in the role of the teacher is a characteristic of constructivist learning.

The material available on the websites for the above courses is quite exceptional: they are part of a pilot scheme in the department of French's Technologies Coordinating Committee (TCC) to integrate technology further into language learning and teaching, with a view to creating Web-based modules in French. One of the main reasons for establishing these programmes seems to be to deal with the needs of increasing numbers of students (these programmes have large numbers of students enrolled on them), by making course material easily accessible to them on the Web. In doing so, this could reduce the need for increased contact time: a similar notion of course delivery was suggested by Blin as part of the SALL (Semi-Autonomous Language Learning) project in Dublin City University (Blin 1995: 51). Other courses, though, provide a substantial range of resources for their students. A series of programmes, entitled 'Language Practice', taught to first, second and third year French, which teaches phonetics and pronunciation, provides a large bank of audio clips, transcriptions and exercises, in addition to pronunciation recordings, such as nasal consonants and linking vowels.

The website for another French course, taught at Mississauga (Introduction to French Studies) contains a comprehensive bilingual vocabulary glossary, a series of skeleton notes of literature lectures, electronic versions of literature texts to be studied in class and copies of exams and grammar tests dating back to 1993, along with model answers. Most of the resources on this website have been designed by an assistant professor of French at Mississauga. A number of colleagues on both campuses provide links to these resources from their own websites, in particular to the on-line grammar notes, which received over sixteen thousand hits between 1997 and 2000. The assistant professor who designed these notes and material has recently designed a pilot Web-based placement test. It is intended that all French students will complete this test so that they can be streamed into classes appropriate to their linguistic ability.

After French, the Italian department at Mississauga is a major proponent of Web-based learning and teaching materials. There, two instructors in particular have created a gateway of links, covering topics from Italian culture to newspapers and radio and television stations, which are available on the departmental website. Two Italian courses, which study Italian Comic Theatre, include video clips on the Italian playwright, Maschere Duemondi. These clips are used as part of the lecture series for those programmes. Furthermore, the department is digitising audiotape accompaniment material for an Italian grammar book, called *Adesso*. This material is available on the first year course website and allows all the students to access the audio files for *Adesso* virtually anywhere and at any time, One of the reasons for digitising this audio material is to avoid the bother of copying endless amounts of audiotapes for distribution among students, ultimately saving time for the technicians involved.

Material in Spanish is more limited. A bank of on-line resources is available on course websites in this subject, these include: translation and grammar exercises, grammar notes, links to radio and television stations, a link to an on-line dictionary and a Spanish verb conjugation tool.

At least two courses (including one in German) provide links to background reading material for some lectures on the on-line programme timetables and students are expected to read the material before attending the appropriate lectures. At present, the German department is digitising the audiotape accompaniment of *Vorsprung* – a course textbook used in the programme entitled: 'Introduction to German' for the same reasons as the Italian department.

CHASS Electronic resources

The Computing in Humanities and Social Sciences service (CHASS) has created an on-line resource centre that incorporates many of the resources and material provided through languages course websites. The centre has created a multimedia database for nine languages, including French, German, Italian and Spanish. The database contains a gateway to Web links for each language. There are over one hundred links for French alone, including links to on-line radio stations and a number of archived articles from Radio Canada, as well as dictionaries and on-line grammar exercises. In addition to this database, the CHASS Resource Centre has created an Audio Gazette for French and Italian, which consists of digitised audio news articles in the two target languages and accompanying transcriptions, recorded each month. The Italian Gazette contains a wider range of audio files than its French counterpart because it was used by Italian teaching staff on the St George campus in their classes in 1999. It does not appear to be used by teaching staff for this purpose any longer, although the material remains in the Italian Audio Gazette for students to use for independent study.

It is hardly surprising that the proliferation of course websites, some of which are interactive, means that staff and students in this institution are highly dependent on the Web.

According to questionnaire findings, a high proportion of staff use the Web. 100% of staff (N=13) confirmed they use the Web frequently for tasks that are not related to University work, while 85% stated they use the Web for University work. This confirms earlier findings showing the existence of an important Web culture among staff, some of whom have their own personal websites and even write Web pages directly in HTML. These findings imply that languages staff at Toronto are generally very interested in using the Web and are therefore are sympathetic to the idea of exploiting it as a teaching and learning tool: this can be seen in the way they use the Web.

When asked how they use it, three important areas were highlighted: to present lecture notes, to research material for class and for academic research. As discussed earlier, 62% confirmed they use the Web communicatively, to present lecture notes and send out class material. Apart from the attraction of using the Web to make material available to large numbers of students with great ease, another reason that may explain why a high proportion of staff use the Web this way is that Web publishing at Toronto is a straightforward procedure. All staff can freely publish on the Web and many languages staff (along with colleagues from the entire Faculty of Arts and Science) are allocated server space and FTP accounts through CHASS. Twelve Web servers are operated by CHASS, providing 420 Gb of server space: this body also provides technical support for staff involved in Web publishing. Furthermore, since a high number of staff use either the University dial-up facility *(UTORdial)* or CHASS dial-up, they can publish files on the University website from home, as well as the office, meaning that they can publish material on the Web at any time, on and off campus. The availability of Web publishing facilities does not, of course, mean that all languages staff publish material themselves: some ask graduate students or departmental webmaster to do it on their behalf.

Substantial numbers of staff indicated that they use the Web for research – both academic and class-related: 92% confirmed they search the Web for class material, while 77% said they use the Web to search for material in their areas of research, such as browsing electronic journals, for example. This finding indicates a general acceptance by Toronto staff of the value of the Web for research purposes. In other words, they consider the Web as a valuable source of reference. In addition, some members of the French department, including two prominent professors, have published articles through a section of the departmental website called the *Net des Études françaises* (NEF). This shows staff willingness to use the Web as a means of presenting their own research, which is a further endorsement of the Web's research potential. The questionnaire discovered that 31% of staff use the Web to design their own language-learning exercises, and a number of these are available through course websites. This percentage seems unusually high because such activities require immense time and effort, not to mention expertise. As a result, many academics simply do not have the ability to be involved in this area of courseware production. Other staff, who have not designed their own exercises, provide links from their own course websites to these exercises or to activities created at other universities. This implies that staff see the potential for using the Web as an interactive tool, as opposed to simply a passive reference resource. Such recognition makes it easier for staff to encourage students to explore the Web's potential.

This can be seen from the results of another question in the survey. When staff were asked how they encourage their students to use the Web, 77% confirmed they ask their students to use on-line language learning exercises, such as grammar drills and gap-filling activities. 85% encourage their students to use on-line dictionaries: this is, in itself, an overwhelming endorsement of Web-based dictionaries, given the perceived limitations in the value of this type of dictionaries for language specialists (Gillespie and McKee 1999a: 40). A number of course websites include hyperlinks to on-line dictionaries, such as the *Dictionnaire Universel Francophone*, encouraging students to complete assignments, usually textual comprehensions, using this dictionary, as opposed to carrying around a cumbersome paper-based one.

The survey revealed also that 77% advise their students to use the Web as a source of reference for researching essay and coursework

164

topics. This can be seen in the format of the first and second year programmes in 'Practical French', where some tutors have included links to reference material on the course website. Students are encouraged to consult the material available through these links to help them answer a series of assessed comprehension questions on-line. 100% of respondents encourage their students to use the Web for self-study, such as reading on-line newspapers and watching news broadcasts in the target language. One of the reasons why such an overwhelming percentage encourages this activity is that it encourages students to experience authentic language being used in a practical context. This is particularly relevant for the vast numbers of students who study the non-specialist language programmes, especially those in French, where students are really interested in learning the communicative essentials of the language. Those students are particularly interested in learning about the everyday use of French, which is often best provided by target language newspapers and television broadcasts, banks of which are easily available on the Web.

Results from the student questionnaire showed that their use of the Web was not exceptionally high overall: 73% of respondents (N=64) use the Web regularly for researching material for essays and other coursework. This supports results from staff questionnaires, suggesting that students are willing to use the Web as a source of reference for their work. Some programmes of study, after all, require students to complete assignments using mainly Web-based resources. This supports the findings of Chapter 3, where curriculum integration was found to be essential in encouraging students to use electronic resources. Using the Web extensively for researching coursework topics can be problematic, however. It may lead to over-reliance on the Web and under-reliance on traditional sources of reference, such as library books. A French tutor at Toronto indicated that if material is not available on the Web, some of his students simply will not search for it in other sources and, on several occasions, they have complained about being unable to complete coursework assignments because reference material was not readily available on the Web. Such a dismissive attitude from students may be the result of over promotion of the undoubted value of the Web, setting it apart from all other sources of information and, by implication, selling it as a more important source of reference. Over-dependency on the Web can cause other problems. In the 2000/01 academic year, the French department at Toronto became very concerned with plagiarism from Web-based sources and, following a meeting of the Technologies Coordinating Committee, all students in French were required to sign a declaration, requiring them to acknowledge all their sources of information, whether Web or paper-based. The fact that this form of plagiarism has become an issue at Toronto shows how extensively students use the Web as a source of reference for coursework.

This does not mean, however, that students at Toronto are enthusiastic users of the Web. When asked if they used it for self-study, such as accessing target language newspapers and radio or TV stations, 27% said they did so regularly. This conflicts with the high percentage of staff who encourage the use of the Web for self-study. Similarly, the overwhelming endorsement by staff of on-line dictionaries and on-line CALL exercises appears to have fallen on deaf ears among students: 28% of them use these dictionaries, while 11% use on-line language learning exercises. Students do not seem to share the staff view that on-line dictionaries, for example, are becoming just as reliable as their more traditional, paper-based equivalents. The gulf between staff endorsement and student usage of the Web is very large – this may be due to the fact that when students are given the option of using it, for self-study, for example, most choose not to use it. This view was expressed during a focus group session with seventeen students from the first year programme in practical French. Although one of the main advantages of the Web is its flexibility, which allows students to engage in self-study at a time and place convenient for them, those in the focus group explained that they felt using the Web is a very time-consuming process and implied that they really only use it is to successfully complete assignments for that course – any additional use of the Web was really unthinkable. Furthermore, they felt the effort required to complete the Web-based assessment was not reflected in the weighting of coursework marks.

In the 2001/02 academic year, the coursework weighting of the Web-based element of this programme was increased to 10%, therefore giving the students an increased incentive for the programme. Nevertheless, results from a student questionnaire, administered by the French department at Toronto in April 2002, showed that there is still substantial resistance to the Web component of the FSL161Y programme.[1] These students are not technophobes – they do not fervently oppose using computers for learning, their reluctance to use the Web is due, in the main, to their discipline of study: practical French. Many of them are taking courses in other faculties, sometimes with a high number of contact hours – they are studying French as an adjunct to their overall degree, rather than as a central part of it. As a result, the time they can afford to spend on their French course, which is less of a priority than their main discipline subjects, is limited. As a result, if the use of computer technology appears to add to their workload for that course, resistance is inevitable. This suggests that the integration of computer technology into a language-learning environment needs to take account of practical limitations that may make it an unfeasible option.

For the specialists in French too, there is little time to use the Web for self-study, due mainly to the fact that most students have part-time jobs to pay their high tuition fees and fund themselves through their degree course. In addition, unlike their counterparts in the UK, students of French in Toronto do not need to use the Web in order to watch target language television or to listen to French radio: there are three terrestrial television stations in Toronto that broadcast in French (some of which broadcast alternately in French and English) and radio stations such as *Radio Canada*, which transmit French broadcasts. This means that students have ready access to authentic target language material without logging onto the Web. This is not the case, of course, for students taking other languages such as Spanish and Italian where students need to use the Web to access such target language resources. Questionnaires for this investigation, however, were completed mainly by students taking French and therefore the results generally reflect opinions, trends and student usage of computer-based resources in that department in particular.

---

1   This can be seen from student comments to question 12 of survey, accessed on the WWW, May 2002: http://www.chass.utoronto.ca/french/frenetica/results_ stud.htm

In addition to the wealth of links to Web-based resources and grammar exercises on course websites, a number of staff in the departments of French, German, Italian and Spanish and Portuguese, have designed in-house CALL programs, with the Italian department leading the way. Two instructors have created a series of CALL programs, including Italian *Hypergrammar, Interactive dialogues* (a series of multimedia video comprehension exercises) and a grammar-testing program. There is, however, an obvious move away from these types of client-based programs and staff are encouraged to use and develop programs written in HTML to be used across the Web. This is particularly in evidence at the Mississauga campus, where the SLLIM project (Second Language Learning Interactive Modules), which in-cludes staff from the French and Italian departments, has provided funding for the conversion of HyperCard-based Italian grammar exercises to HTML. In the French department at Mississauga, there were nineteen local CALL packages for French in 1994, available in multimedia labs on campus; in 2001, there were two packages. This ratio is similar at St George, where there were six networked CALL programs in the multimedia labs in the 2000/01 academic year. Some staff are developing their own Web-based exercises: in French, a bank of three hundred self-correcting grammar exercises is being created and in German, staff are developing a Web-based grammar theory exercise and have already developed a series of self-correcting gram-mar exercises, using *Hot Potatoes*.

On the St George campus, the following local client-based French programs are also used: *French Pronunciation Tutor, Paroles Francophones, Rapport Now, Hyperbase* and *Wordcruncher* (which are literature analysis and database programs). *Paroles Francophones* is used alongside Web-based exercises created within the department for pronunciation practice in the modules FSL181, 281 and 381Y. Paroles Francophones is one of two networked CALL programs avail-able in the multimedia labs at Mississauga, along with a textual com-prehension and writing program, called *Ecrit*.

Although there is a shift towards Web-based CALL, one local client-based CALL program is used extensively, especially in the

French department – *Le Correcteur 101:* a spelling and grammar checker. The Italian department uses a similar package called *Errata Corrige 2.5*. Furthermore, multilingual versions of MS Office 2000 have been installed in the multimedia labs, offering target language spelling and grammar checking capabilities. Staff encourage students to use these checkers in spite of the obvious concern that students will become too reliant on these proofing tools and their grammar and spelling will suffer. In fact, one of the first pieces of software to be installed on the computers in the multimedia labs at Mississauga when they were first opened in 1995 was the French version of WordPerfect with French spelling checker. Those members of staff who encourage the use of these proofing tools require students to check the spelling and grammar of their coursework using these applications before they submit it (and are encouraging colleagues to make the use of these tools compulsory for their students too). Some of these instructors, although not all, will then penalise simple orthographic and grammatical mistakes in students' coursework with greater vigour than they would if their students' did not have access to the proofing tools.

The most commonly used client packages available in the multimedia labs are sound and video players, such as *RealPlayer*, *Windows Media Player* (used to watch video clips or listen to audio passages, especially target language broadcasts) and *PureVoice*, which serves as a digital audio recorder, used for pronunciation practice. Another recording package, called *WinPatch*, helps to improve students' accent and articulation in the target language through graphical representation and syntheses of their voices. With the exception of *WinPatch*, the rest of these packages are freely downloadable from the Web and do not require expensive site or lab licences and, moreover, they are not restricted to use within multimedia labs, unlike the CALL packages discussed above. This means that students can use them in the College dorm over the University network or in private accommodation, using a modem. Given the dispersed nature of the University of Toronto, it is not surprising therefore that these types of programs are being used in preference to locally networked packages because of their flexibility.

CALL packages are limited in Toronto: Web-based material is more common. In fact, before staff and student questionnaires were administered, it was decided, upon the recommendation of departmental staff, to avoid using the term 'CALL programs' in questionnaires because it would seem alien to many of the respondents. Instead, they were asked to give details of any language packages that they used, including networked and Web-based packages. Results from the student questionnaire reflected limited usage of local CALL software.

Questionnaire results showed that students use the grammar and spell checker – *Le Correcteur 101* – although the percentage who admitted using it was very low. A total of four respondents (6.25% of those who completed the questionnaire) admitted using it. Three of these students said they use the grammar and spelling checker independently of class, while only the fourth student said he uses it as part of class-related activities. This low usage is quite surprising considering that some staff, in particular those on the Mississauga campus, require their students to use *Le Correcteur 101* to check the spelling and grammar of essays and other written work before submitting them. One might imagine that students would be very willing to use this piece of software because of its obvious value for eliminating thoughtless typing mistakes in their work. Its lack of use indicates that even when the pedagogical advantages for using computer technology are obvious, this does necessarily guarantee extensive use.

Voice recording packages such as *PureVoice* and the phonetics program *WinPatch* are used more frequently: a total of nine students said they use these packages – especially for class work. No other local CALL package was mentioned by students. These figures indicate that, overall, the use of local CALL programs is quite insignificant at Toronto.

In view of the fact that 69% (N=13) of staff encourage their students to use these CALL packages independently of class, this makes the figures outlined above seem even more dismal. The student questionnaire revealed that ten respondents (16%) attend the multimedia labs for independent study, implying that they use language-learning programs for autonomous learning purposes. In other words, the findings here show, once again, a large gulf between staff encouragement to use electronic resources independently of class and the number of students who actually do so.

170

One reason that may explain this low use of local CALL packages is that most of these packages can only be accessed in the multimedia labs and the satellite multimedia room in the Kelly Library. This means that students cannot access them across the Web, which, given the high level of off-campus student access to the Web, would seem a more flexible and possibly popular option, allowing them to use the packages whenever they want and whenever they have the time to do so, rather than being constrained by lab opening hours. Once again, this shows the importance of ensuring the use of technology is not impractical, even when the pedagogical advantages are obvious. Whereas Le Corecteur 101 is recognised as a very useful piece of software, students can only access it in multimedia labs on campus. For many students, it is often impractical to visit these labs every time they want to check the syntax and grammar of their written French. The lack of flexible access is one of the reasons why staff are not encouraged to write local CALL packages but rather to design them in HTML or using Web templates such as *Hot Potatoes*. This raises an interesting, if controversial issue. Burnage (2001: 169) argues that a rush towards developing Web-based CALL may overshadow the generally more functional locally networked packages. As a result, CALL developers are faced with two choices at present: to design CALL courseware in Web-based format and therefore lose some aspects of functionality, such as instant access to audiovisual files and clips, or to design networked packages that maintain all these features but do not offer the same flexibility of access as the Web. The view adopted at Toronto seems to be that less is more. In other words, staff and students can live with the loss in functionality of CALL packages if it means that they will be more accessible and can be used on any computer, both on and off-campus. Nevertheless, since students do not necessarily make extensive use of Web-based resources that provide them with the flexibility they are looking for, it is difficult to imagine that any local CALL packages redesigned for use on the Web will actually be used by many more students, especially if they are expected to use them for private study. Perhaps, however, one way of ensuring that CALL resources are more widely used, aside from making them more accessible to students through the Web, for example, is to address the problem of student time pressures. At present, students have very limited time to use CALL resources outside class time – a reduction in the number of class contact hours may afford students the necessary time to experiment with CALL. Since many students have classes in other faculties and departments outside modern languages, however, any restructuring of class contact hours would need to be implemented across faculties and departments.

Multimedia labs

The Computing in the Humanities and Social Science service (CHASS) provides a number of computing labs on the St George campus. There are two open-access labs: one located in the Kelly library and the second in the basement of the Bissell building, where CHASS is situated. These are general-purpose labs that students can use for checking their e-mail, typing up and printing out essays and other generic tasks. There are also four dedicated multimedia labs, one satellite room in the Kelly Library and two small Research and Development (R&D) labs used primarily but not exclusively, by the languages departments. These labs are controlled by a division of CHASS known as the Multimedia Centre for Learning in the Humanities and have a total of one hundred and forty-two computer workstations. This centre is responsible for software provision in the multimedia rooms and installs and maintains the types of CALL packages and other multimedia programs discussed above. Likewise, the rooms provide access to networked dictionaries for twelve languages, including *Le Petit Robert* and the *Oxford English-Spanish* and *English-German* dictionaries, all of which are networked through the Library. Faculty staff and graduate students use the R&D rooms to test out new programs on a small scale before the centre installs them on the lab machines. The multimedia labs are primarily a teaching facility – they are not open access and although they provide a range of generic programs, like Microsoft Office, there are no printing facilities and only staff or graduate students with swipe cards can use them outside teaching hours. The largest of the multimedia labs, situated in Carr Hall, with thirty PCs, is booked for teaching purposes over twenty-five hours a week (around twenty hours per week for language classes). A smaller lab, situated at University College, with around twenty PCs, is used just under twenty hours per week (of which around fifteen hours are language classes). The labs are therefore very busy, although, in an effort to reduce the number of classes taught in the labs each week, two additional labs were built – one in the Kelly Library and one in the extreme north-west corner of the St George campus – during the 2001/02 academic year.

These new labs have not yet been extensively used for teaching because staff and students are not fully aware of their existence. During periods when the labs are not being used for teaching, students can only use the rooms if there is a supervisor present (these supervised sessions amount to two or three hours per day). There are no supervised sessions in the evenings because some of the multimedia labs are hired out for two or three evenings each week to another faculty: the revenue generated by this is used to purchase new software or peripherals. The satellite lab in the Kelly Library, created in the 2000/01 academic year, is dedicated to private study and no classes take place in it. For a number of courses, students are required to use the main multimedia labs for self-study and their attendance at the labs is registered by monitors on duty. Their attendance in the labs during the monitored supervisory sessions can count towards coursework marks in a number of courses. In one German course, students are given the opportunity to make up for class absences (if they have more than two unexplained absences, coursework marks are deducted) by spending time in the multimedia labs for private study.

In addition to the multimedia labs at St George, there are two interconnected multimedia rooms at the Mississauga campus: these labs are not run by CHASS but rather by the Faculty of Arts and Science at Mississauga itself. One of the labs is a dedicated Mac lab, with fifteen new G4s (mainly used by two members of the Italian department for their HyperCard-based CALL programs). The other has over thirty PCs. Unlike the labs at St George, these rooms are open access and teaching hours are limited to four hours per day in the larger lab and two hours in the Mac lab. This gives students plenty of free slots to use the labs and, if one lab is being used for teaching, the other will always be free. There is always a supervisor or technician present, either at a help desk or in an adjacent office. Unlike at St

George, where there is a wealth of computers all over campus, there are just over one hundred and sixty PCs (including both multimedia labs) for student use on the Mississauga campus and so if the multimedia labs were principally used for teaching purposes, student access to computers at Mississauga would be very more limited because there are so few other labs that they can use.

Staff, therefore, have access to six multimedia computer labs over the two campuses and they use them for a variety of teaching activities. Some instructors in the practical French programmes give their students a series of questions, based on units they study in a textbook. Students are required to search the Web to acquire more contextual and background information in order to answer the questions fully. These programmes generally require students to spend one of the three weekly contact hours in the multimedia labs. Apart from using the Web to enhance reading and writing skills, students are also required to use the labs to enhance aural and oral skills. A common class activity is pronunciation practice, using *PureVoice* or *WinPatch*. In these types of classes, students follow an activity sheet or work on exercises and use resources that have been provided on the Web, through course websites, for example. Other staff provide students with a series of questions based on a video or audio clip that the students view or listen to through *RealPlayer*, with the option of pausing and replaying clips and consulting on-line or networked dictionaries. In some of these classes, the tutor is more like a facilitator of student learning, directing them towards particular resources. Other instructors prefer to play a more central role in the class activity, rather than that of a supervisor, and they work through activity sheets or lead discussions based on video or audio clips.

One course at the Mississauga campus was based almost entirely on activities in the multimedia lab. This course was an e-mail writing exchange between students at Mississauga and French-Canadian students at Glendon College, York University, situated north of Toronto. Students were assigned a tandem partner and they were required to maintain bi-weekly e-mail contact with their partner, using their target language. The U of T students would type out an essay in French dealing with a topic that they covered in class, reviewing a film or book, for example. They would then use their next class in the multimedia lab to edit or improve the composition, with guidance from the instructor, check the spelling and grammar of the work, using *Le Correcteur 101*. Finally, they would then send the typed composition by e-mail to their partner at Glendon College, who would respond with comments or suggestions (Besnard, Elkabas and Rosienski-Pellerin 1998: 385–94). The main purpose of this exchange was to focus on differing writing styles in French and the students' tandem compositions made up the coursework mark for this module. This course ran for four years, between 1992 and 1996 and the module has now been replaced by a larger and more wide ranging course called 'Language Practice II: Written and Oral French'. This type of initiative is an example of how the computer is used to facilitate learner participation and interaction with one another. It follows Piaget's theory that interaction includes and extends beyond the classroom (Elkabas *et al.* 1998: 247). The use of electronic communication allowed students to interact with one another both inside and outside the classroom.

Importance of the multimedia labs

These labs provide languages students and staff with a vast bank of computing facilities, ideally suited for audiovisual work. The provision of this level of hardware and software seems essential in the process of establishing the computer at the heart of the language learning and teaching environment at Toronto. Furthermore, judging by the number of hours they are booked for teaching purposes each week, staff and students are utilising this expensive technology. Such an observation is confirmed by the results of the staff questionnaire, which discovered that 77% of respondents (N=13) take classes in the multimedia labs and 69% encourage students to use the facilities independently of class. Results from students, however, reveal a very different side of the story.

When students were asked how often they used the multimedia labs, 59% (N=64) said they have classes in the labs, reflecting staff results for the same question. On the other hand, however, a vastly reduced proportion of students (16%) said that they use the labs for independent, private study. The question also showed that of the ten respondents who use the labs independently of class, two of them (20%) said they use these labs on a regular basis. Students on some courses, including those who responded to the questionnaire are often required to use the labs independently of class in order to obtain a coursework mark. They may have considered this as an extension of class work and not independent study, explaining the low percentage who admitted using the labs for self-study. Nevertheless, the results of the question reveal that, given the choice, students do not use the labs. There are two reasons for this.

Many of the language learning exercises that students use are Web-based: some of the material that is not, like *PureVoice*, are easily and freely downloadable from the Web, allowing students to use them on their own PC. Furthermore, the range of packages that are only locally available in the multimedia rooms is very limited: the most useful of these would seem to be the spelling and grammar checkers but, as the questionnaire findings showed, these are not used as extensively as might be expected for such valuable pieces of software. Furthermore, even if students use the grammar and spell checkers in the labs on the St George campus, they cannot print out their work there. Instead, they must go to one of the general-purpose labs or one of the libraries to do so, taking up more of their time, which, in turn, could completely discourage some students from using the spell and grammar checkers.

Since the multimedia labs on the St George campus contain a vast range of expensive equipment and are located in different University buildings across the city, security is a major issue in these rooms. Access to the main labs is controlled by swipe cards and students can only use the labs when no classes are taking place in them if one of the supervisors is present. This means, inevitably, that access to the labs is very restricted and students are usually unable to use the labs at times that are convenient to them. Quite often, students want to use the labs in the evenings or at weekends, but cannot do so. In addition, most multimedia labs are located in areas that are not very central for students.

This differs considerably from the location of the multimedia labs on the Mississauga campus, which are situated in the heart of the

North Building, near student facilities such as the cafeteria and within a very short walk from most classrooms and lecture halls. On the St George campus, students quite often have to trek a long distance to the multimedia labs and, given the busy class schedule for the labs, they are often unable to use the facilities. The new labs on the St George campus, as well as the satellite multimedia room in the Kelly Library were created to ease this problem of access, however since they are all new installations, it may take a few years before their benefits are felt. This satellite lab in the Kelly Library is located in an area where there is a lot of student traffic and operates the same opening hours as the Library. Somewhat paradoxically, since it is located in a communal area for all students, it is likely to be heavily used for general tasks such as printing out work or checking e-mail and therefore students who want to use local packages such as *Le Correcteur 101*, may find themselves prevented from doing so.

These reasons contribute to the high level of student reluctance to use the multimedia labs on the St George campus, supporting Levy's argument (1997: 202) that the integration of computer technology into teaching and learning is hindered by the problem of making computers available to students when they really need them. In addition to being reluctant to use these labs, students also appear openly resistant to them. Many react with hostility at being compelled to use the multimedia labs as part of their coursework without sufficient access to them. This means that they are required to use labs at times that are not convenient to them, when they can ill afford the time to do so. This observation is supported by the results of the student question-naire. Half of the 16% of respondents who confirmed they use the multimedia labs for independent study, were students from the Mississauga campus (students from that campus made up only 16% of the total number of respondents to the questionnaire – 10 out of 64). This indicates that the proportion of students who use the labs for independent study on the Mississauga campus (where labs are conveniently located and are open access) is manifestly higher than the percentage that do so on St George. In other words, students will use the labs when the physical and psychological barriers that inhibit their use are removed.

The use of multimedia labs at the University of Toronto is clearly a complex issue. They play a pivotal role in the development of Web-based learning and programmes of study. The fact that students at the St George campus do not use them as much as either they or staff would like them to means that the labs are not as important to the student learning environment as they could be. Multimedia labs on the Mississauga campus are more 'student-friendly' and this is one of the reasons why the labs there are more central to the student learning environment on that campus. It is evident that administrators and directors of the multimedia labs at St George can learn from the success of the Mississauga labs. However, since St George is a vast campus, spread across downtown Toronto, it will prove difficult to change the *status quo* of the labs there and to make them a more integrated part of the student learning experience. There remains some work to be done before the cybernautical model suggested by Elkabas *et al.* (1998: 247) from the French department at the U of T, which advocates the elimination of the traditional divide between working in the computer lab and working in a conventional classroom, can be achieved in this institution.

Learning approaches

The use of computer technology in this institution allows for both a constructivist and behaviourist approach to learning. The use of multimedia labs for directed teaching activities, such as web searches and phonetics classes, is an example of behaviourism in practice, while the use (or at least the invitation to use) these labs for self-study is an example of constructivism. In addition, the Web-based learning modules in Practical French are examples of the integration of behaviourism and constructivism, with the opportunity for self-study and active learning, although within the control of regular, teacher-led classes. As a result, computer technology plays an important and useful role in facilitating the type of balanced learning context discussed at the start of this thesis. Consequently, the computer does not replace the human teacher, but rather redefines his role within a language-learning environment.

178

Planning a computer-based language-learning environment

Computer technology is already used very extensively at Toronto, which, in itself, suggests that the University has planned its language-learning environment around computer technology, although other indicators demonstrate this too.

Role of management: ensuring computer competence

University management have attempted to develop an e-culture in Toronto and establish computer technology at the heart of the learning and teaching process. This can be seen in the level of computer literacy within the institution.

One of the simplest ways of measuring standards of computer literacy is to evaluate the level of computer training that staff and students need and receive. There are three main forms: Faculty-wide and University training in the basics in computing and induction provided at course or departmental level for specific software applications or other electronic language-learning material.

Since faculty-specific computing services like CHASS take care of the daily management of computing facilities, it follows, therefore, that training languages staff and students ought to be the responsibility of CHASS. This assumption, though, is increasingly inaccurate. CHASS did provide an induction course for all faculty students in the basics of computing (Applied Certificate in Computing in the Humanities): this course existed until 1999. It was stopped, among other reasons, because of dwindling attendance (although those who completed it successfully received a certificate, this was not a recognised qualification). Furthermore, with over twenty-five thousand students in the Faculty of Arts and Science, it was a Herculean and impossible task to provide the financial and human resources needed to offer training courses to all students in the Faculty. Inevitably, places on the course were severely limited, meaning the numbers who completed the course were only a fraction of the numbers in the Faculty.

Similarly, CHASS organised several well-attended workshops for staff, dealing with issues like Internet and e-mail basics, along with more advanced topics like Web publishing. These workshops took place in 1997 and were one-off events, although the notes from the sessions are still available for consultation on-line through the CHASS website.

In recent years, there has been a move away from this type of faculty training. Information Commons now provides information packs for students when they enrol for e-mail, in addition to on-line tutorials that deal with e-mail and Internet basics. On the Mississauga campus, too, Computer Services provide on-line tutorials for students there. This change in induction policy also reflects the view that students are perceived to be very computer-literate and do not need induction in the basics of computing like e-mail and word processing. Whereas, it is obviously difficult to prove this theory, the numbers of students with access to their own PC off campus seems to support this view. A University-wide survey on computer use in 1999/2000 discovered that 91% of U of T students had access to a computer in their own home.

Limited training is provided for staff. A division of Information Commons, known as the Centre for Academic Technology (CAT), offers regular workshops each semester for staff. These are not general induction courses, instead they are intended to show staff how to use technology in their teaching effectively, examining particular packages, such as *WebCT* or HTML editors like *Dreamweaver*. They provide examples of good practice, rather than a basic induction. These sessions target more technologically advanced members of staff, as opposed to the computer novices. This suggests that many staff are already very computer literate and do not need extensive training. Colleagues, however, do not share this view and a mere 15% of questionnaire respondents (N=13) felt they were well trained in the use of computer technology for language teaching and learning.

Languages departments provide more specialised training in the use of the computer for language learning. French and Italian, in particular, provide computer courses for their students. These courses, which last a full semester, are only available on the Mississauga campus. The French programme – Teaching and Learning French with

180

New Technology – teaches the use of e-mail, word processing in French, design of Web pages, use of grammar checkers *(Le Correcteur 101)* and basic programming. The course is available to third year students only and is therefore not marketed as a basic induction course, suitable for example for first year students and newcomers who have just arrived at U of T and need training in the use of the computer for language learning purposes.

The Italian department at Mississauga offers two computer courses: one is a third year course, 'Testing and Evaluation of Language Resources', along the lines of above French programme, and a postgraduate module, entitled 'Computer-Assisted Language and Literature Teaching in Italian'. Both courses deal with advanced aspects of computing in languages and provide more than a simple induction to the department's computing facilities. The content of the third year Italian programme has been modified over recent years, from dealing with the basics of e-mail and the Web, to more complicated areas like analysing websites and evaluating grammar and other proofing tools, as well as the use of e-mail for language learning. The advanced content of these courses is further evidence of the University-wide belief that students are already very computer literate. They show students how the computer can be a central part to their language learning process and encourage them to make maximal use of the computer for this purpose. In other words, the courses show the computer as a normal part of their language learning process. The provision of such courses is therefore important to the integration of the computer into a language-learning environment. However, they are only available to a limited number of students for they are not compulsory modules. Furthermore, they are only available at the Mississauga campus and not at St George, which is clearly the larger campus, where most of Toronto's language students are based and, therefore, where there is more potential to use computer technology in language learning. Consequently, departmental efforts to integrate ICT into its language-learning environment through the provision of computer language courses are not as extensive as they could be: a more central computer training approach in the languages departments on both campuses is required.

Since computer literacy among students is thought to be very high, it follows students in the U of T feel quite comfortable using the computer. As a result, induction and training in the use of computers does not appear to be a major factor in the integration of computer technology into the students' learning environment of U of T.

Role of management: ICT integration

One factor that plays an important role in achieving this integration is the role that the computer plays in the everyday life of the University.

The U of T operates a Web-based student records system called ROSI (Repository of Student Information). When they log in, students have access to a range of facilities, including course enrolment details. Students register for their programmes of study electronically through ROSI. There is no cumbersome matriculation process, where students have to queue up to fill in forms. Upon completion of the necessary fields on the ROSI database, the information is transmitted to the main student records system. Once they have enrolled on all their courses and the academic registry processes the information, timetables are automatically created and each student's unique timetable will be posted on the ROSI system as well as their examination timetable. Similarly, students can use ROSI to check the cost of their student fees and, if they are paying them in instalments, they can check on the outstanding balance. Students use ROSI throughout the year: they can use it to change enrolment for courses (within a limited time period) and can check their current grades for courses. In addition to being used for academic purposes, students can use ROSI to vote in the elections for the Student Administrative Council (SAC), which is similar to the Students' Union in the UK.

The ROSI system is therefore a very important and central part of university life at Toronto; it encourages students to use the computer regularly for everyday matters, not just for academic information. Given the size and decentralised nature of Toronto, it is quicker to send out administrative material electronically than by conventional postal methods. By sending out individual timetables through ROSI, students have access to this information virtually anywhere and do not have to go to a central point or noticeboard to collect this information.

ROSI is only part of the wider electronic environment at the U of T: the Library too has an important role in it. The main U of T Library (which does not include college libraries) operates an advanced electronic environment. Firstly, in the 2000/01 academic year, the Library joined forces with Academic Registry to provide a joint University smart card. This means that when students enrol for the first time, through ROSI, they will not receive a student card. They must then, however, register at the Robarts Library, where they will be issued with a borrower card that doubles up as a student card. This, of course, is not a new concept and many universities have used a common student/library card for a number of years. However, unlike other cards, this new library card contains a microchip. Students can use this smart card in photocopiers, printers and even in vending machines in the Library and elsewhere to purchase snacks and drinks. They can top up their credit themselves through dispensing machines: all cards are provided with CAN$100 credit and if students use more than that, they must pay for the credit top up. The smart card is also known as the T-card. In addition to the above functions, student can use it to check out library books themselves, using self-service computerised library terminals, avoiding large queues at the issue desks.

The T-card represents yet another step towards the integration of computer technology into the daily life of the U of T students. The card is used for various purposes, many of which are everyday common tasks, including buying food. Furthermore, the card gives students good flexibility: they can top up the print credit themselves at any time, for example. On the Mississauga campus, until recently, students did not use a card to print out in the computer labs; instead, they were allocated printing credit through their personalised desktop login. One of the major disadvantages of this was that students could only top up their print credit at Computer Services helpdesks during office hours and this meant that, if a student ran out of print credit after that time, he would have to abandon the printing job until the next day. Using the T-card, students can top up their print credit outside office hours, removing the inflexibility of the previous system.

This is a further sign of the removal of the types of hardware problems that have often caused levels of student resistance to ICT in the past.

The Library provides students and staff with a wide range of electronic material. This includes an electronic examinations database, giving access to examination scripts from the past ten years. The scripts are available in electronic format across the Web, allowing students to consult them from home, their College dorm or a computer lab. Students, therefore, have easy access to this information, without the need to even visit one of the libraries.

Similarly, the U of T library contains the largest collection of electronic information resources in Canada. There are over thirteen thousand electronic journals, six thousand e-books and two hundred licensed newspapers and news services available through the U of T library website. Although many of the journals are science-based, there is a wide range of material relevant to the modern linguist, including electronic books dealing with such topics history and culture, as well as literature material. Due to licensing arrangements, this material is not openly accessible across the Web and can normally only be accessed from computers on the U of T network. However, the Library makes these resources available to users outside the University network through a proxy server, meaning that staff and students can access the material from home, using an ordinary modem and Internet Service Provider. This type of flexible access to resources is particularly important for the many U of T students who need to juggle their academic studies with having a part-time job. In most cases, students will use this material for researching essays or other forms of coursework, as well as revising for examinations and, as a result, it is particularly advantageous for these students to have 24-hour access to a wide range of library material that they can consult at times suitable for them, late in the evening when they finish their part-time job, for example. From a student's perspective, it may seem more important to have access to these types of resources because they are considered essential for completing coursework. Other Web-based resources such as on-line language learning exercises and target language material are not necessarily considered by students as essential for successful course completion.

The Library, therefore, operates a highly computerised environment, but it does not end there. The U of T's library catalogue provides a comprehensive computerised database that, in addition to being used as a searchable index of library holdings, allows students to check the status of their loans and renew them, if necessary. The library has adopted an e-mail notification system for overdue books, recalled material or billing notices. Although this is not automatically available to all students – they must register for it by completing an on-line form – those students who receive e-mail notices are not sent any hard copy correspondence. This means that the Library is beginning to use e-mail as its main means of communication with staff and students, thereby giving the computer a central role in everyday University tasks.

Computer technology, therefore, is used in a wide range of daily (and mundane) tasks at the University. The computer seems to be a natural part of the university environment and, by extension, of the students' learning environment.

Management support: technical infrastructure

If the computer is to become an integral part of the learning and teaching environment, provision of adequate facilities is a necessity. In this institution, computer facilities are of a high standard, although they are not perfect. Responses to the staff and student questionnaire show that 70% of students (N=64) and 54% of staff (N=13) believe they have computer facilities that are adequate for their use of ICT. Although levels of satisfaction are generally high, one of the common complaints from students is that there are not enough computers for all students (remembering, of course, that the U of T has more students than any other Canadian university).

The role of management in providing better computer technology to meet these needs is essential. Recent initiatives such as leasing contracts between the University and hardware companies led to the refurbishment of the multimedia labs on the St George campus during the summer of 2001, thereby improving the reliability of the equipment in those rooms. Other projects, including negotiations with computer companies to provide banks of laptop computers for Arts students and possibly even an on-campus laptop repair centre are being initiated. When implemented, they will enhance the level of computer provision among students.

The University already has an excellent support infrastructure in place to help staff integrate technology into their teaching. In the Faculty of Arts and Science, CHASS provides a comprehensive full-time technical support service to repair staff and student computers on the St George campus. The multimedia labs on both campuses now operate a helpline facility, usually staffed by graduate or final year students, who are paid by the Faculty for their time. This type of technical support provided is obviously very extensive and, according to King *et al.* (1998: 15), it is essential in ensuring the successful integration of computer technology in the learning and teaching process.

Staff in the Faculty at St George have access to the Information Commons multimedia suite, as well as some electronic publishing facilities in the graduate multimedia lab. They can use these facilities to prepare material for Web publishing, including audiovisual resources such as films or interviews. Furthermore, in the suite at Information Commons, staff are offered training and help when they use the multimedia editing equipment. This makes it much easier for staff to prepare their own websites and course material and may also explain why the use of the Web has become so prolific at Toronto.

Another example of this support infrastructure can be seen at departmental level where graduate students have been employed on a part-time basis by at least two languages departments to work as webmasters, uploading material for course or departmental websites on behalf of academic staff. In the department of French, two web-masters have been employed on one campus. One designs and maintains the departmental website and the other monitors course websites and uploads material to them on behalf of staff who do not have the time or knowledge to do so.

Similarly, the department of French benefits from a yearly subscription to the resources of *Universia* – the educational division of Radio Canada, which provides a digitised archive of its radio broadcasts in French over the past sixty years. This facility gives staff access to a vast bank of digitised target language audio material that they can use for listening comprehensions or other class activities, usually providing password-protected links to them on their course websites. Languages staff on the Mississauga campus will also shortly be able to benefit from a digitised audio library, created by one of the Faculty technicians there. This library will contain all target language audio cassettes used by the departments. It means that staff do not need to spend endless hours digitising their own material. Access to *Universia* is a privilege available only to Canadian institutions and material is available only for French. Nevertheless, it serves as a model for other countries, including the UK, where these types of vast banks of digitised material are not available to all institutions, usually because of copyright limitations.[2]

These initiatives and mechanisms for supporting staff in the integration of technology into their teaching have been made possible by management at University, Faculty and departmental level, who have adopted a policy of employing support staff (usually graduate students) and providing high quality equipment. This requires considerable funding and the fact that management are prepared to spend millions of dollars each year on human and technical resources shows a considerable commitment on its part to supporting the use and integration of computer technology into teaching and learning.

Management support: academic credit

Support from management has also played an important role in raising the profile of staff who have been involved in development electronic courseware and other similar initiatives. This support comes from departmental, Faculty and University-level management.

Staff who are interested in developing computer-based projects are often eligible for financial support from provostial sources in the form of either the Instructional or Courseware Development funds.

---

2   In the UK, the British Universities Film and Video Council (BUFVC) provides subscribing institutions with access to a bank of target language video broadcasts in VHS format only.

Initiatives in the French department have benefited from this support: one example is a project at Mississauga to rewrite some local-based CALL programs on a Web-based template. The provision of these funds sends out an important message to staff concerned in such projects. The University values the efforts made by colleagues in integrating computer technology into teaching and learning and is prepared to show the seriousness of its commitment to their initiatives through financial investment.

Support has been provided by the Dean of the Faculty of Arts and Science, who has shown interest in many of the computer projects undertaken by departments, especially the French department. His enthusiasm in this area has been very important when departments have sought funding for some of their projects. During research meetings at central University level, he has frequently drawn attention to articles published by staff in the area of ICT other related fields. This demonstrates that he and, by extension, the Faculty he heads are willing to support this type of research. The current Dean of the Faculty shall shortly be stepping down from office but indications suggest that his successor will be equally enthused by the use of computer technology in teaching and learning. One of the reasons why both the Faculty and the central University have supported computer-based initiatives is that they further enhance the excellent research reputation of the institution.

Support at this level varies across departments. The French department is a good example of how staff have been encouraged to develop the use of computer technology in teaching and learning and engage heavily in research in this area. Three research groups were set up: *FRENETICA* (Cours FRE: l'Enseignement et la Recherche enca-drés par les Nouvelles Technologies de l'Information, de la Communi-cation et de l'Apprentissage); *RECALL* (Research at Erindale into Computer-Assisted Language-Learning) and *NEF* (Net des Études françaises). While the first two groups are involved in researching the use of computer technology in teaching and learning, the third group is mainly involved in the development of computer-based research in other aspects of French language such as the creation of an on-line corpus of the works of Voltaire and Lamartine, as well as designing an on-line concordance of the *Dictionnaire de l'Académie française*.

188

Another example of the esteem in which the department holds research and work in computer technology is the fact that, in May 2000, the department hosted a prestigious international conference, entitled: 'Les études françaises valorisées par les nouvelles technologies d'information et de communication'. Amongst the keynote speakers at this conference was Robert Peckham, the creator of the 'Tennessee Bob's Famous French Links' gateway of Web resources.

Other departments, though, have not really shown a similar form of support for colleagues engaged in work and research in the use of computer technology. This is best illustrated by the example of one department where a research student, who had initially started her PhD by examining levels of technophobia among language teachers was advised by the Chair of that department to change her approach because it was felt that this type of research would not lead to a job there.

Despite a very comprehensive management structure that is clearly supportive of efforts to advance and develop computer-based language learning, there is little evidence of an actual policy in this area. In the French department, for example, it is apparent that most interest and impetus for developing the use of the computer in teaching and learning comes from the professors and departmental staff. The creation of the TCC (Technologies Co-ordinating Committee), chaired by two professors and made up of departmental tutors, is an example of this grassroots support. The Chair of the department is very supportive of such initiatives: she has published articles in an area related to the use of computer technology in learning and teaching and suggested that the French department host the international conference, mentioned above. The former Chair, too, was very supportive and interested in this area. The role of the Chair in encouraging computer-based language-learning and teaching has been mainly practical – seeking funding for necessary hardware, software and human resources, rather than implementing a common ICT policy. There is little need, though, for such a policy to be implemented by the Chair because it is obvious that there is enough impetus from her junior colleagues to encourage other departmental members to use ICT in teaching and learning. Furthermore, the initiatives and projects created by French staff have inspired colleagues from other departments, such as Spanish and German, to start their own projects and use computer technologies in ways that they have never considered before, whether out of pure interest in this area or because they feel compelled to keep up with the technological developments of their French counterparts.

Support from the chalk face

When asked whether or not they consider the use of ICT beneficial for language learning, staff responses were positive, although cautious. Many seemed to share the view that the use of ICT is conditionally beneficial, 'if planned and used intelligently'. Some cited access to a wide range of resources, especially across the Web, as one of its main attractions, while others said that students expect ICT to be used and, by implication, that the staff have a duty to meet their demands and even use it more in class. In response to another question, 31% of staff respondents said they believed students want an increase in the use of ICT in class. At least three respondents expressed a feeling of unease when using computers in the multimedia labs, believing that when the computers break down or things seem to go wrong, this makes the staff look incompetent in front of their students. One of these respondents said he feels that classes in the multimedia labs are not really productive for students who do not always focus on the class activities because they hide behind the computer screen and e-mail friends or surf the Web for personal entertainment. This type of student behaviour suggests further evidence of resistance and resentment at being compelled to use the multimedia labs, although, more than likely, it simply confirms the view of Burgess and Eastman (1997: 163), who believe that students associate the Web with play rather than work. The concern expressed by this member of staff highlights the need for more planning of class activities in the multimedia labs and also suggests that staff do not yet feel they have completely and successfully integrated ICT into their language teaching – only 15% of them said they feel that their department is using ICT to maximal effect.

190

The responses from students were also cautiously positive. They too cited many advantages to using computer technology, including many already mentioned by staff. In addition, some added that ICT has enhanced student-staff communication and leads to better use of class time because lecture notes and other material are posted on course websites. Students, though, were clearly mindful that its use does not and should not mean the elimination of regular personal contact with tutors, suggesting that they are concerned that the use of computer technology will isolate them from the teacher. Questionnaire responses from students in one focus group to the question about the value of ICT in language learning showed they felt that too much emphasis was placed on the use of computers – they were expected to research and complete assignments on-line – and this had discouraged most of them from wanting to use computer technology further in their language learning. The views of these students echo those of Kohn (1995: 18), who argues that the use of computer technology in language learning and teaching ought to be driven by user need and therefore not for the sake of it. It could be argued that if students saw that the use of computer technology was beneficial and directly relev-ant to their language learning, these feelings of disillusionment would be less noticeable in all but the fervent technophobes.

The overall attitude of students and staff towards the value of computer technology in language work was enthusiastic and this would suggest general support at a grassroots level for the creation of language learning and teaching environment based around computer technology at Toronto.

Course structure

The positive reaction expressed by languages staff and students to-wards the use of ICT is influenced by the way that technology is made integral to the curriculum at Toronto.

There is a wide range of language courses on offer in Toronto. Computer technology lends itself to inclusion in the delivery of many courses. The multimedia labs, for example are used for phonetics practice, aural practice and exposure to other forms of authentic target language material, all of which are particularly important in the vast range of practical French language courses that the University provides. Nevertheless, in some of more practical language-orientated courses, such as the heavily technology-driven, FSL161 Practical French course, extensive use of ICT is not always suitable. These types of language courses focus on using the language for practical purposes, usually in conversation. As a result, students on this type of course require a considerable level of personal interaction. If high ICT content is to be retained, it seems more appropriate to provide enhanced computer-mediated interaction, through synchronous forms of communication such as chat rooms or live video chats.

Many courses across the languages departments reward students for working at computers. This is clear from the high proportion of staff who require their students to use language-learning programs in the multimedia labs regularly, in order to obtain a coursework mark. A similar method of rewarding students is through the use of grammar and spell checking software, where some staff use a deliberately more stringent marking system to correct work because they expect their students to check the spelling and grammar using this software before submitting the work.

Another example of linking course evaluation to computer use is the establishment of computer-based testing. In both French and Italian, computerised placement tests are being piloted to stream students into suitable classes. In addition, the University is experimenting with computer-based examinations. At present, students in a Masters degree programme in the French department on the Mississauga campus complete one of their exams on computer. They use either their own personal laptop or a PC provided by the department. Encouraging students to use their own computer does not compromise security in these exams. They are permitted to save notes onto the hard drive if they wish and are actually advised to do so because examiners give them a list of the subjects that they will be tested on in advance of the exam to allow them to prepare for it. They do not know, of course, in advance what focus the exam question will take and are tested on their ability to manage all the information they have collected, as opposed to simply regurgitating data. Obviously, if any of the language departments were to allow computers to be used in undergraduate exams, the numbers of students involved would make it impossible for departments to provide computers for each student, unless each student had his own laptop. This means that the extension of computer-based examinations to undergraduate language courses at Toronto remains unrealisable, at least for the near future. However, its inclusion in some examinations shows that there is potential for using ICT in that previously unexplored area.

Both staff and students are keen to develop computer-based language-learning, which is supported by the flexibility of course structures in languages. As a result, there are few obstacles inhibiting the development of a computer-based language-learning environment and this seems to explain why computer technology is used so extensively in the process of language learning and teaching at Toronto.

Chapter Six
Success or failure? Meeting the needs of learners and teachers

Computer technology plays an important role in each of the case study institutions: the extent to which each one has created a computer-based environment is less clear and this needs to be examined in context of the user requirements described in Chapter 2: technical, psychological and organisational. Furthermore, it is also important to consider how the use of the computer in each institution meets the pedagogical needs of learners and teachers in its roles as a tool, tutor and resource.

Technical requirements

If students and staff are expected to use computer technology for language learning and teaching, it is important to have a high standard of equipment. Each of the universities studied in this investigation offer a different range of computing facilities. The way in which these facilities meet the needs of staff and students can be assessed in two areas: the provision of a networking infrastructure and the provision of computer facilities dedicated to language learners

Global Access

If students are expected to make extensive use of electronic resources, such as dictionaries and CALL packages, as well as using e-mail to communicate with staff and even submit work electronically, access to the Internet or local networks is essential and, furthermore, it is important that access be flexible enough to allow them to use such resources late in the evening or when they have no classes. Rigid opening hours in computer rooms often mean that students cannot access computer facilities when they wish and when they can gain access, sometimes they have to queue to use computer facilities.

The provision of networking infrastructure is an important aspect of the learning environments described in this thesis. In Cambridge, access to network resources from college bedrooms has proved essential in integrating computer technology into daily University life. It may help to explain why students, for example, are regular users of e-mail and, consequently, why e-mail has become the preferred means of communication in the Faculty of Modern and Medieval Languages. This network system enhances the language-learning environment at Cambridge by providing an infrastructure that brings computer facilities closer to the language students and links together most of the computerised language learning resources and tools. One of the problems with this system is that languages students are frequently unaware of (or do not feel it necessary to use) the resources that are available to them, in spite of extensive efforts by MML staff to make students aware of this material. This suggests that the creation of an infrastructure to provide electronic resources is not enough to ensure their widespread use (McCartan and Hare, 1996: 22). Users need to feel the infrastructure is relevant to them and enhances the learning and teaching experience.

Whereas the networking system clearly provides a valuable infrastructure for the language-learning environment at Cambridge, this approach does not work in other cases. Both Ulster and Toronto require a more flexible approach to ensure that students have access to electronic resources in term-time accommodation. At Ulster, however, unless there is some way to ensure that those students have better Internet access in their term-time, privately leased accommodation, it is difficult to see how the Web could offer an effective infrastructure that links together all parts of the language-learning environment. This demonstrates that there will not be a common infrastructure for each computer-based environment, such as the Web or a local network, which will meet the needs of students and staff. In some cases, it may

196

be very difficult to use the computer as an infrastructure to disseminate information and resources. The only way to ensure its effectiveness as a infrastructure may be to ensure that all students have their own computers, possibly connected to the Internet may be to use cellular phones to dial up to an ISP, or, possibly to a subsidised university dial up facility that would ensure that the operating costs of such a system are not too prohibitive for students.

Dedicated facilities

Cambridge and Toronto provide dedicated computer lab facilities in an effort to integrate computer technology into language learning and teaching; the University of Ulster installed such labs in the summer of 2002. Whereas the CALL Facility at Cambridge is a modern installation, it is not used to maximum effect for self-study and teaching purposes. This contrasts with the labs at Toronto, where overuse, especially for class activities, has led to very restricted access for students who want to use them for self-study. A number of reasons have been offered to explain why the CALL Facility at Cambridge has not yet proved to be a central part of the language learning and teaching experience. These reasons support the argument for ensuring that a computer-based environment is considered relevant to staff and students and that technology is suitably integrated into learning and teaching practices.

One way to ensure a more natural integration of the labs is to locate these labs in a socially central area for learners and teachers. The Macintosh lab on the Coleraine campus of the University of Ulster (now replaced by one of the languages multimedia computer labs) was an example of how suitable location contributes to making the computer an everyday part of the learning and teaching experience. Although this lab was not specifically dedicated to language learning and the technology there was certainly not cutting edge, the lab was located in the area of the médiathèque. This meant that the lab was located in a central area for students – allowing it to become a social hotspot for students to meet up and chat. In other words, students would feel less isolated when using the computers in that lab than they seem to feel in the CALL Facility at Cambridge and in multimedia labs on the St George campus at Toronto. Locating these facilities in a socially central area is more feasible on a small campus, such as the Coleraine site at Ulster where almost everything is situated in the same building, than on a disparate campus like Cambridge and Toronto. Nevertheless, in both these institutions, efforts are being made to address the issue. In Toronto, the installation of two new multimedia labs – one for private study and the other for class – in the Kelly Library is an obvious attempt to locate facilities in a socially central area. In Cambridge, plans have been made to convert part of the former English Library in the Raised Faculty Building (RFB) into a social area for students, offering catering facilities and an area for students to meet up and chat. It is hoped that, by drawing students into this social area, students will be attracted to the CALL Facility, which is located nearby and that they will feel less isolated about using the Facility. At present, though, Ulster seems to offer more scope for the natural integration of languages computing facilities into the learning and teaching experience there, even though its facilities are not yet as developed as in the other institutions.

Another key factor is the integration of labs into learning and teaching processes. In Toronto, for example, the labs are widely used for teaching purposes, especially for aural work and textual comprehension. One of the main reasons why the computer labs are used for this purpose is the ready access to a vast range of target language audiovisual and textual materials. Students are also required to use these labs for independent study because many programmes of study have linked the use of labs into coursework evaluation procedures. This means that the languages computer labs in Toronto are considered a key part of language learning and teaching there, especially in the development of reading and listening skills. The CALL Facility in Cambridge does not appear to have the same relevance for staff and students there. Although this Facility is used for teaching, students are mainly encouraged to use it for self-study and for examination revision. As a result, there is a perception that students do not need to use the resources and material available in the CALL Facility to successfully complete most of the University language degree courses.

Partee (1996: 79) believes that computer technology needs to become invisible and therefore blend into the background so that staff and students focus less on the technology and more on its pedagogical and didactic value. One common characteristic of the labs in Cambridge and Toronto is that their integration into the learning and teaching experience is quite artificial. In both institutions, students have to make a special effort to use the computer facilities to enhance their language learning and, in Toronto, they use it in order to receive coursework marks, for example. Stepp-Greany (2002: 175) argues that this is a valuable way of encouraging students to attribute relevancy of work and educational benefits to technology-enhanced instruction. Although, it seems that students do not always make a natural association between using the computer labs and language learning. If they did, students in Cambridge, for example, would be more willing to visit the CALL Facility regularly to enhance their language learning and would overcome the problems that they associate with using the Facility, such as having limited access to generic software there. This illustrates that a crucial aspect in the development of a computer-based learning environment is the development of a learning culture. This would encourage students to use computer facilities with the same readiness and lack of inhibitions as they would use other facilities, such as a library. If students need to consult a book, they go to the library partly because that is what they are trained and encouraged to do and partly because they know that it is pedagogically beneficial. The example of *FirstClass* at the University of Ulster shows the value of such a learning culture. There, server difficulties mean that the *FirstClass* system is not very reliable, yet students see beyond its shortcomings and use it regularly because they recognise it as a clearly valuable part of their language learning and are widely encouraged by many staff to use it, who themselves have enthusiastically adopted the system for disseminating information and facilitating communication. Far from feeling compelled to use it, many students actually seemed enthused by it.

Psychological requirements

Achieving a high quality technical infrastructure is clearly important for staff and students. A number of psychological issues also need to be addressed. Each institution has dealt with these factors in different ways.

Support mechanism

Both Cambridge and Toronto have appointed dedicated staff to develop the use of computer technology in language learning and teaching. These staff include graduate students, full-time technicians, Web masters and CHASS support staff. That does not mean that academic staff cannot use the technology themselves but it means that the more technologically challenged members of staff do not need to concern themselves with the technical aspects of uploading course material and, instead, they can concentrate on developing material, writing course notes and finding useful reference links. Although not all the staff mentioned above are dedicated Modern Languages staff, the availability of various members of technical support staff means that each one can specialise in particular areas, such as Web authoring, digitising audiovisual material and repairing hardware. This avoids duplication of roles and improves the efficiency of such a support team.

The appointment of several technical staff to look after the computer needs in languages is not a luxury available at Cambridge. Whereas this university has appointed a full-time CALL Officer, several staff have been appointed in Toronto to carry out these same duties. He is not responsible for fixing technical problems in staff offices or in the student labs – a Faculty technician takes care of such problems. The Language Centre in Cambridge has a team of technicians who have similar duties to the Faculty CALL Officer. These staff are, however, not part of the Faculty and aside from occasional areas of collaboration, such as digitising banks of video comprehensions, the roles of the CALL Officer and Language Centre technicians remain separate. Although the MML Faculty is considerably smaller than its Canadian counterpart, the appointment of one CALL Officer is clearly inadequate to meet all the demands of staff. This means that courseware development and additions to software in the CALL Facility are not always addressed as quickly as they would be at Toronto. This has undoubtedly discouraged some staff from developing courseware and gives the impression of an insufficient computer support infrastructure.

If the technical support infrastructure at Cambridge can be described as deficient in comparison to a seemingly slick system at Toronto, the Ulster infrastructure is non-existent. Ulster does not provide a systematic approach to this area. There are no dedicated CALL staff who are responsible for developing courseware and assisting staff with the transfer of course material to electronic format. Any support available comes from a limited number of graduate students and faculty technicians, whose main responsibility is the maintenance of staff computer facilities and faculty computer and audiovisual equipment. Academic staff, therefore, have to develop courseware and other electronic materials themselves. A number of staff have developed CALL software and transferred course notes to electronic format on their own using *FirstClass*. They are, however, the real enthusiasts, who will press ahead with the development of computer-based learning and teaching regardless of obstacles. For the more pragmatic adopters of technology, who are generally in the majority, developing courseware on their own is too time-consuming and requires more technical expertise than they either have or are prepared to learn (Gillespie and Barr 2002: 131).

The examples of Toronto, Cambridge and Ulster show the necessity for a comprehensive technical support mechanism if computer technology is to become established at the centre of the language learning and teaching process. This support mechanism does not simply mean the appointment of one or two CALL Officers or similar staff, it involves a team of specially dedicated staff: such a team will also consist of technicians to fix hardware and software problems. This supports the view of Burnage who argues that 'it is the dynamic combination of expertise which yields the best results' (1999: 13). The mechanism in Toronto appears to be very efficient and this has considerably enhanced the development of computer-based language learning. Obviously, few institutions, not to mention Modern Languages departments or schools could afford to appoint such a comprehensive team and, for this reason, it may be more appropriate to pool resources. Cambridge is a good example – the expertise of Language Centre technicians in digitising audiovisual material is clearly beneficial to the MML Faculty. With closer links between the two, this would allow the CALL Officer to transfer some of his heavy workload to the Language Centre technicians, perhaps leading to greater efficiency in courseware development. Furthermore, by using staff already employed by the University, the MML Faculty would not need to create additional full or part-time posts to meet this need. In the Ulster case, too, the ability to pool resources with other faculties or borrow staff from other areas, such the Institute of Lifelong Learning (whose staff will assist in the transfer of course material to WebCT), would be a useful way of ensuring that there are enough staff to assist the creation of languages courseware and resources. This solution, however, could only be an interim measure, postponing the inevitable need to appoint someone to co-ordinate the development of a computer-based language-learning environment.

Training

Whereas the three case studies provide differing levels of technical support in languages, ranging from efficient to virtually non-existent, the universities share a similar approach to staff and student training in the use of computer technology in language learning and teaching. In all three, training is not systematic.

Out of the three institutions studied, Cambridge provides some training to all MML students, through an introductory lecture on the CALL Facility and computerised language-learning resources. One of the main difficulties with this lecture is that it cannot attempt to cover all necessary aspects nor will students absorb everything that they are informed about in such a short session. There are few follow-up sessions for most students. The main reason for this is a lack of time and a poor response from most students who are often unwilling to attend training sessions that bring them no apparent value (academic credit, for example). In recognising this problem, Cambridge now offers an accredited computer course that lasts for a full academic year – the Certificate in Humanities Computing for Languages (CHUCOL). Toronto and Ulster adopted a similar idea years earlier, providing modules and programmes, which form part of University degree courses, dealing with the use of computer technology in language learning. All these courses, however, only target a limited number of students and it is not possible to provide places on these courses for all students in Modern Languages. This has led to a situation where some students will understand the value of using computer technology in language learning, as well as having a high level of computer competency, than other students in Modern Languages who are not able to complete these courses.

Staff training too is not systematic in any of the institutions. One-off seminars are usually the most that each of the institutions can offer, mainly because of the difficulty encouraging staff to attend training sessions during term-time as a result of heavy teaching schedules. In each institution, staff can attend generic training sessions, provided by computer services or staff development departments. These sessions, although arranged into a regular training program, also find it difficult to encourage staff to attend. Furthermore, such sessions are essentially generic and, consequently, they do focus specifically on the integration of computer technology into language learning and teaching. The arrangements for staff training in Cambridge, Toronto and Ulster are far removed from the model suggested by Kassen and Higgins (1997: 269), who advocate a systematic training programme for language teachers. Such a model is perhaps a little utopian because of the difficulties getting staff to attend these sessions. A possible solution is offered by Cambridge, where the MML Faculty Board is considering the possibility of extending the CHUCOL to staff also. This would give staff a sustained training programme and also reward them with an academic certificate, which they may find useful when applying for promotion or teaching positions in other institutions. Given the time constraints that many staff face, it could be more realistic to offer web-based training programmes, such as the ICT4LT course, which they could complete in their own time. Creating such a model highlights the importance of introducing a clear staff training policy that managers and heads of department are prepared to implement in an effort to ensure better staff awareness of the potential of computer technology in language learning and teaching.

A common feature of the computerised resources and facilities in the three case studies is that they are continually evolving and developing. If students are provided with training in their first year at university, by the time they reach final year, a host of new resources and facilities will have become available to them and they will probably be unaware of these new developments. As a result, training students effectively in the use of computer technology in language learning will not take the form of a one-off course or series of classes. It seems important for sustained training to be provided in all years of study, as well as among staff, introducing new ICT developments when necessary. In the three case studies, there was little evidence that such sustained training was on offer. Some final year students in Cambridge, for example, were unaware that they were able to access CALL programs and server-based dictionaries from their college bedroom because these facilities were not available when they were first trained in using the CALL Facility.

The issue of staff and student training is problematic in the three institutions. It appears obvious that a comprehensive training framework has not yet been established to ensure that all students and staff are given adequate and regular training in the use of computer technology in language learning and teaching. Staff and students in each case are becoming increasingly computer literate, especially in Cambridge and Toronto. Evidence of this can be seen from the percentages of both groups who use computer technology, such as e-mail, the Web and generic software regularly for personal use (the percentage of staff who use e-mail for personal use, for example, was 92% in Toronto, 85% in Cambridge and a more reduced 62% in Ulster, N=13, 42 and 13 respectively). Increasing computer literacy could be one of the reasons why training has not been given more consideration in each institution. Nevertheless, it does not guarantee that students and staff appreciate the value of using ICT in language learning and teaching: specialist training is still necessary.

Integration with non-academic facilities

In addition to developing the use of computer technology in language learning, each of the institutions are also developing initiatives to integrate computers in everyday university life, although some of the initiatives appear more successful than others.

Ulster and Toronto have developed a Web-based electronic student records system. These electronic information systems have proved to be particularly useful because they offer staff and students the flexibility to access this information on and off campus. This is particularly beneficial for staff who may need access to student records while working off campus, and for students, who may want to check out examination results, for example, from home during the summer vacation. The availability of these facilities also encourages the use of computer technology for everyday tasks. By making this type of administrative information available on-line or in some other electronic format, students and staff become increasingly reliant on using computer technology to access it. The provision of electronic information management systems, therefore, plays a pivotal role in the development of an e-culture among students and staff.

In all three universities, there is a wide range of electronic library resources available. The availability of e-journals and other library material across the Web (such as databases and dictionaries) are particularly beneficial for the Toronto context since sizeable numbers of students commute from home each day to university. At Ulster, there is a wide range of electronic library resources available, although students there cannot benefit from the full advantages of such electronic facilities because of limited off campus Internet access in term-time. Access to library facilities is obviously less of an issue in Cambridge because students live quite close to the University and college Libraries. Nevertheless good network access in college bedrooms makes the availability of electronic library resources particularly attractive there in comparison to the other institutions.

Electronic resources are not simply beneficial for students; staff can also benefit from them. In the three case studies, high numbers of staff have access to the Internet from their own accommodation. The availability of electronic library resources therefore gives them greater flexibility to access reference material, either for class preparation or in pursuit of research interests.

The creation of a bank of electronic resources and information management systems demonstrates the institutions' commitment towards using computer technology to simplify aspects of everyday life at university. Ulster and Toronto are continuing their development in this area, (the creation of Campus One at Ulster is an example). This is further evidence of the development of an e-culture, which encourages students and staff to rely increasingly on computer technology. One might argue that the institutions' desire to develop such electronic resources has created staff and student reliance on such facilities in the first place and that was not driven by apparent need or demand from either group. Sometimes, however, institutions must take these measures in order to persuade potentially reluctant or resistant staff and students of their benefits.

Organisational requirements

Each institution provides support and an organisation infrastructure for efforts to create a computer-based environment. There are two forms of such support: implicit and explicit. Implicit backing includes support for colleagues involved in ICT initiatives and adequate reward for their efforts, such as research recognition or due credit at times of promotion. Explicit backing involves such areas as specific policies and initiatives that encourage the integration of computer technology in the learning and teaching process. Both forms of support have manifested themselves in different ways across the three institutions and this leads to important conclusions being drawn about the level of commitment and desire to integrate computer technology in this way.

Implicit support

This form of backing was found to be lacking in Cambridge, in particular. There was an obvious lack of academic recognition for ICT projects, especially at MML Faculty level. Staff involved in developing computerised courseware felt frustrated at their efforts failing to be recognised at times of promotion, for example. In addition, the Faculty focuses on research in literature and linguistics: the area of CALL and associated research topics simply do not seem to fit into its research ethos. This has sent out a clear message to staff interested in developing electronic courseware and other e-learning initiatives as the basis for research projects. The value of such work is not recognised by the University as proper research. This attitude is not exclusive to Cambridge: many other institutions in the UK have adopted similar approaches. There are, however, signs that attitudes towards this area of research are changing. In the 2001 Research Assessment Exercise (RAE) in the UK, the Unit of Assessment in French, for example, accepted publications in language pedagogy, which includes the development of new electronic courseware, among the evaluation criteria.[1] Some of the staff who are involved in ICT research in the MML Faculty are obviously impassioned by their work in this area and continue their projects and research regardless of a lack of systematic support. For those who could be described as the pragmatic enthusiasts however, a lack of academic credit is problematic. This group of staff is willing to become involved if they feel the work involved in developing ICT initiatives pays off, both pedagogically and in terms of research. Consequently, it would appear that a lack of implicit support for such work is discouraging some from getting involved in CALL and ICT. This leads to another problem: with few staff involved or likely to become involved in this work, the impetus for encouraging and convincing others, such as the rigorous opponents of the use of computer technology in language learning and teaching, loses momentum.

1   See RAE Panels' Criteria and Working Methods, available on the Web at: http://www.rae.ac.uk/pubs/5_99/ByUoA/crit51.htm

This is certainly not the case in Toronto, where the efforts of the French department have inspired other Modern Language departments to embrace the use of computer technology. In that institution, research and efforts spent developing ICT projects are being rewarded through research recognition and, more specifically, through the creation of research bodies dedicated to ICT research. The creation of such research bodies sends the clear message that research in this area is as real and valid as other areas of research, such as literature. Many of the staff involved in this research and the development of ICT initiatives are key members of staff, such as well-established professors and chairs of department, past and present, and their presence adds to the impetus and kudos of such work.

The University of Ulster has a similar level of support to Toronto. Research in the area of ICT is recognised and given due credit and senior staff have been involved in this area of research. At the same time, considerable impetus for the development of computer-based language learning comes from the Head of School, as opposed to the grassroots impetus that exists in the other cases. Nevertheless, one of the main failings of the implicit support for computer-based language learning is that there are fewer staff involved than in the other institutions. This has weakened the momentum of the impetus that encourages the development of computer-based language learning at Ulster.

Explicit support

This type of support exists in all the institutions, although it is more apparent in Ulster and Toronto. In both cases, there have been a number of developments in policy that have encouraged the spread of computer-based language learning. Ulster seems to provide the most focused support. Both the senior management of the University and the School of Languages and Literature have adopted a consolidated approach. In the case of the University management, this can be seen from the development of the Campus One on-line learning initiative. At School level, attempts have been made to formulate a policy regarding the use of computer technology, such as the use of electronic communication. Financial restrictions and considerations affect the implementation of such a policy, suggesting perhaps that greater impetus is needed from higher levels of management to actively seek more funding.

In Toronto, there are obvious efforts to establish a policy for computer-based language learning (this is part of the brief of the Technologies Co-ordinating Committee in the French department). In addition, senior management support has been evident through the availability of several sources of funding for ICT initiatives and facilities, such as hardware and software for the multimedia labs. Unlike Ulster, however, policy varies across the Modern Languages' departments. Historically, these departments have been separate bodies in the Faculty of Arts and Science, unlike in Ulster where all the languages are co-ordinated by the School of Languages and Literature, which is part of the Faculty of Arts. This means that some languages department in Toronto will have more developed and focused policies in the area of computer-based language learning than others. The French department's ambitious policy of creating Web-based programmes of study in the FSL161 and 261Y courses is an example of such an approach. Furthermore, it explains why some of the developments in the use of computer technology in language learning and teaching, such as the use of course websites to disseminate information to students, have not been uniformly adopted across the departments. Some departments preferred to let others take the lead in this area and then if their initiatives proved successful and worthwhile, they would follow suit. In recent years, Toronto has made efforts to co-ordinate the policies of each department, through the establishment of the Language Department Consortium. One of their most recent achievements has been to create an on-line collaborative research forum, developed using WebCT. At present, though, the Consortium has not addressed the issue of a common ICT policy and it looks likely that such a policy will not be realised in the near future. This body, though, seems best placed to achieve the coordination needed for such a policy.

Cambridge lacks the type of policy that Ulster and Toronto are developing. Most of the efforts to develop ICT initiatives have normally taken their impetus from one or two individuals and not from a central policy. Most of the impetus tends not to come from further up the management hierarchy, although University bodies have provided hardware and software funding, which suggests the institution's willingness to use ICT. Lack of funding to appoint extra support staff, on the other hand, indicates that this policy could be seen as slightly myopic because, as already seen, computer technology on its own does make the difference, it needs staff to maintain and ensure its effective use.

From their respective efforts to develop a policy for computer-based language learning, it seems that Toronto, as in many other aspects, is ahead of its British counterparts and it has demonstrated sustained institutional commitment to the development of a learning environment based on computer technology. Ulster, though, is best placed to develop a policy that all Modern Languages there will adopt and, as a result, has also shown an encouraging level of commitment towards using ICT in language learning and teaching. Putting this policy into practice is more problematic. Cambridge has the financial capability to implement such a policy but has failed to sustain its implementation – this is perhaps an indication of the nature of that institution's governance, which seems to make it more difficult to establish a computer-based language-learning environment than in the other two institutions.

Course design

There is a strong correlation between the design and structure of Modern Languages courses in the case studies and the development of the use of computer technology in learning and teaching there. The content of language courses in each institution affects this development.

This has proved a decisive factor in the successful integration of computer technology in Cambridge. In this institution, the Modern Languages degree courses offered by the MML Faculty do not require the use of CALL and ICT. Students are expected to use CALL packages and other programs to develop their language skills outside class. Furthermore, students and staff alike in Cambridge perceive CALL as an exclusively language focused activity and this has led them to question the value of using CALL to complete many MML courses where literature is the major strength. There are, however, encouraging signs that this perception may be changing, since there are more first years than finalists using CALL packages. This suggests that CALL is being accepted more into MML courses.

One of the main problems remains, however, that CALL work is not directly assessed as part of the MML degrees. Some moves have been made to introduce a certain level of continuous assessment to MML courses, and this could be decisive in attaining better CALL integration into the curriculum. Most staff, however, who ask students to use these resources are dependent on the self-motivation and foresight of students to realise that this work ought to improve their language competence rather than on their desire to achieve continuous assessment marks. At the same time, however, language courses taught by the Language Centres have proved more successful in integrating CALL. On-line grammar and vocabulary exercises and activities are an essential part of the non-specialist Cambridge University Language Programme (CULP). In other words, students must complete these activities in order to successfully complete the CULP. That programme, of course, is specially designed for on-line learning, and it is more difficult to change existing MML course structures to include greater use of computers. Nevertheless, it illustrates how curriculum integration is vital if ICT is to play an important role in language learning environment.

In Toronto, course content is less problematic. In Toronto, students have regular classes in the multimedia labs, where they use language-learning programs and material that are relevant to their language courses, such as phonetics and aural exercises. Using this type of material is regarded as a pivotal component on the U of T language programmes and students know they must use the technology in many courses in order to obtain coursework marks. Furthermore, students are encouraged to use Web-based resources, such as reference material, to research essays and prepare assignments (links to such material is often provided from course websites). Students in Toronto, though, appear less motivated to use computer-technology because of the benefits it brings to language learning than their

211

Cambridge counterparts. They are driven, instead, by the pressures of obtaining the maximum amount of coursework marks possible.

Ulster seems to offer a naturally more favourable course structure than the other two universities. As in Toronto, the use of CALL packages, such as *MetaText*, is directly assessed as part of some French modules. Furthermore, students are regularly advised to use the Web in order to research essays or prepare presentations on area studies or other contemporary topics. Ulster does not have the same extensive assessment mechanism that Toronto has adopted to ensure the integration of computer technology into language learning and teaching. This integration, however, is occurring naturally anyway. That does not mean, however, that students in Ulster are driven by a lesser desire to obtain maximum marks possible in modules than their Toronto counterparts. Some students involved in the recent tandem language-learning Châteauroux project were primarily motivated by the desire to obtain good coursework marks for that French module; students in *MetaText* class made similar comments. Students have demonstrated a willingness to use technology when it brings them obvious benefits – using the Web to research essays and, more recently, the generally enthusiastic response to on-line grammar diagnostics tests are evidence of this.

If the use of technology is seen as peripheral, it is hardly surprising if students do not wholeheartedly embrace its use. It can be argued that most students in any university are driven by the desire to obtain the best possible marks in their overall degree and therefore enhance their employment opportunities. If they are expected to put in extra effort to use computer technology for preparing work, for example, they will want some recognition for this. As a result, the successful linking of computer technology into coursework evaluation procedures appears just as important a factor in establishing a computer-based learning environment as any other factor discussed here.

Pedagogical requirements

Each environment uses the computer in different ways in the process of language acquisition. There are three main ways that computer technology has been used: as a tool to enable communication, as a tutor to teach language through CALL packages and as a resource, providing staff and students access to a wide range of reference and target language material. In each university, there are different pedagogical demands placed on these three elements and this has affected the way in which computer technology is integrated into the language learning and teaching process.

Computer as a tool

The cases studies revealed that the computer is heavily used as a tool to facilitate communication between staff and students. In Cambridge, e-mail fulfils this role; at Ulster, *FirstClass* has done so for staff-student communication, with e-mail being adopted for communication between colleagues. The Web has been adopted for student-staff communication in Toronto, and e-mail is used between colleagues. In each case, electronic communication has proved essential to keep in contact.

In the Cambridge and Toronto examples, students and staff are spread across a wide area too, often in different buildings and colleges. Fast and efficient communication is essential to ensure that staff and students can therefore keep in contact with one another across a wide area. Electronic communication has proved vital in these institutions, boosted by good term-time Internet access. In Ulster, since campuses are quite small, students and staff are not as widely dispersed. As a result, hard copy communication remains quite commonplace and effective at Ulster, more so than in the other two cases. Electronic communication has, however, proved its value in that university by enabling staff to keep in contact with students when at their home address or on study abroad, in particular. As a result, communication in each institution has been enhanced by computer technology. In all cases, electronic communication allows staff and students to keep in contact outside the normal confines of class contact hours and even off-campus – a feature that is especially relevant in Toronto.

The computer is used for sending and receiving work. In all institutions, the practice of sending and receiving work electronically is not as popular as using e-mail and other forms of CMC for general communication. It seems to be most common at Ulster than in the other cases, especially when *FirstClass* is used for this purpose. In the institutions, one of the main complaints against receiving work electronically is the time and effort required to either print out students' work or to mark it on screen. From the students' point of view, this system has some merit. In all cases, students could save time travelling to staff offices (sometimes across cities) to submit work – time that they could productively use doing other work or even some self-study. Nevertheless, unless staff can be persuaded that using CMC for the electronic submission of work will enhance language learning and teaching procedures (just as it has vastly improved general staff-student communication), it seems unlikely that staff will embrace it with great enthusiasm. Some would argue that there is no value in reducing the burden on students if it means adding this burden to staff!

This suggests the need to develop a culture of electronic work submission. It already exists at Ulster, having developed through students' and staff dependence on *FirstClass*. This type of culture does not exist at Cambridge, where the prevalence of handwritten work and small group supervision sessions makes electronic work submission somewhat superfluous. Toronto, too, does not seem to possess such a culture, which contrasts to the generally enthusiastic adoption of computer technology in many other areas of language learning and teaching there. The adoption of Web-based bulletin boards for electronic submission of work in some French programmes at Toronto is evidence, though, that such a culture may be emerging. Just as it took several years for the fruits of the *FirstClass* culture to emerge at Ulster (the system was introduced in 1996 and its use really exploded in 1999), it may take a few years for the same to happen in Toronto. This shows that a computer-based learning environment is developed gradually: changes in pedagogy and in tradition take time to filter through to all (or even the majority) of staff and students.

Computer as a tutor

CALL programs (both local and Web-based) are used in each university in the role of a tutor. The availability of such packages varies in each case study, although Cambridge and Toronto have most programs, whereas Ulster is presently developing a bank of the packages.

In all three examples, CALL programs are used to give students practice in aural, reading and written aspects of the target language, such as grammar, translation and phonetics work: they are generally not used to develop oral skills in the target language. The under-use of CALL in this area is obviously intentional because of the lack of oral spontaneity offered by such packages (Levy 2000: 182). In two institutions, the computer is used for teaching support, giving the computer a secondary role in the process of language acquisition; while only Cambridge seems to use it in a primary teaching role, through the use of CALL packages for self-study. In each case, therefore, CALL can be seen as a way of using the computer to consolidate the role of the human teacher, which supports Levy (1996: 241). The low use of CALL for self-study purposes is apparent in all cases and this confirms Gillespie and McKee's view (1999b: 45) that this form of independent learning simply does not happen. In all cases, there was evidence of a relatively high level of staff encouragement to use CALL in Cambridge and Toronto and low numbers of students who use CALL outside class. This proves Fox's belief (1997: 5) that students often fail to make use of the learning opportunities afforded to them. This implies that the poor acceptance of CALL among students does not necessarily mean that students feel uneasy with or unsure of computer technology and are therefore reluctant to use it. It suggests, however, that students tend to lack the motivation to use any learning resources, unless its use is a course requirement. Given the low usage of CALL computer technology seems an unlikely replacement of the human language teacher just yet, although the use of CALL software has enabled the human teacher to take on another role. When these programs are used as part of class activities, tutors often seem to adopt the role of learning facilitator and guide, helping students use the software effectively. As a result, the use of CALL software in class has led to a shift from teacher-centred to learner-centred learning activities.

Computer as a resource

In the institutions, the computer is probably used most of all as a resource for class related and self-study activities. Students and staff use computers to access a number of different resources that they use to prepare class work. In Toronto and Ulster, the Web has proved particularly useful for staff and students as a source of reference because it contains a wide range of political and cultural information that is particularly relevant to the languages curriculum of both universities. In Toronto, for example, the creation of Web-based modules, which require students to use computer technology to prepare and submit work electronically, necessitates the use of the Web to complete assignments. The use of hard copy material to prepare assignments for these modules can actually often prove more time-consuming than using the Web. In Cambridge, on the other hand, it is perceived that these types of resources are less relevant in the curriculum and this explains why fewer students use the Web for coursework research.

Students can also access other material on computer: staff in these universities provide lecture notes and support material, either on the Web or on *FirstClass*. The provision of such material is more prevalent in Ulster and Toronto than in Cambridge. In the three case studies, presenting lecture notes electronically is clearly useful for students, providing them with supplementary notes and sometimes simply more detailed information. It also allows staff to present material quickly and effectively to largest possible target audience (such as different classes studying the same topics).

By using electronic resources, such as the Web, students in each institution have access to target language material, such as newspapers. In Ulster and Toronto, where students enjoy considerable exposure to the target language in class, electronic target language resources provide students with additional exposure to the language. In Toronto, students can easily access most of this material on and off-campus across the Web, therefore allowing them the flexibility to engage in self-study at convenient times, late in the evening, for example. Ulster does not use computer technology to provide this type of audiovisual material: the bulk of its resources in this area are analogue – available on VHS or conventional audiotape, although the arrival of the new languages computing rooms will necessitate the development of such material in digitised format. The value of digitised resources in Ulster is, however, more questionable than in the other two cases since access to such resources off-campus, across the Web, for example, is problematic for students living in term-time accommodation. Like with CALL, though, the use of electronic resources for self-study is not always high, which is further evidence that students do not always make good use of the learning material that is available to them. One reason for this may be the high level of exposure to target language in classes, which may lead to a lack of student appreciation of the value of such materials outside class.

In Cambridge, these resources are particularly important since students receive more limited exposure to the target language in class. The use of such resources helps to make up for the lack of exposure to such material in the core curriculum. Furthermore, electronic banks of audiovisual material, such as digitised listening comprehension examinations and transcripts, are prolific in Cambridge. Since this material is available on the local network, students have the flexibility to access this material in their college bedrooms or computing rooms at any time and therefore can use it for self-study when it suits them best. This explains why more students in Cambridge use electronic resources for self-study than in the other cases. In other words, students in that institution seem to have a better understanding of the pedagogical value of this material than in the other two cases.

Constructivism versus behaviourism

Each of the environments discussed in this book facilitates learning in different ways. In Ulster and Toronto, behaviourist and constructivist learning takes place in those environments. In Chapter 1 it was discussed that the most effective approach to learning is one that combines constructivism and behaviourism: a combined approach to learning is not just beneficial for the learner but it is also important to achieve the integration of technology into many aspects of learning and teaching. In Cambridge, computer technology tends to facilitate constructivist learning and, consequently, the computer is not used extensively in classroom activities there.

Conclusion
A framework for an effective environment

At the beginning of this study, three research questions were asked:

1. What is a 'computer-based language-learning environment'?
2. What is involved in the creation of a computer-based environment?
3. Are such environments necessary? Do they work?

In answering these questions, a number of main conclusions can be drawn.

What is a computer-based language-learning environment?

A learning environment is composed of four main elements and a computer-based environment integrates technology into each of these areas. It is used as a resource, as a tool, as a means of facilitating communication between all those who use the environment and as part of the infrastructure that links together all other areas. An environment dedicated to language learning uses computer technology in these ways to teach students the four main skills of language acquisition: speaking, listening, reading and writing.

A computer-based environment does not mean that the computer is the only aspect of it. The main role for this type of environment is to enhance the teaching and learning experience. For language acquisition, this means enhancing the types of learning and methods discussed in chapter 1. Enhancement does not mean the replacement of existing effective pedagogy. In some areas, such as the use of CALL packages for grammar work, for example, the computer replaces existing pedagogy. In doing so, however, it frees up the tutor to teach other areas of language acquisition, thereby enhancing existing forms of pedagogy. If technology does not enhance teaching and learning, it does not need to be used.

This study has discovered that a model computer-based environment does not yet exist, although some institutions are nearer to achieving one than others. This means that a computer-based environment that works well in one institution will not necessarily work in another. Furthermore, in some cases, course structures, tradition, cultural factors and facilities mean that the development of a model environment is often impractical.

What is involved in creating an environment?

The diverse nature of each university means that it is difficult to establish a common set of steps to be followed in creating a computer-based environment. There are, however, a number of key factors that should be considered in creating a computer-based environment.

Technical sufficiency

Computer facilities need to be of a good standard. In addition to this, however, sufficient access to computers, printers and a comprehensive e-mail system is needed to ensure that it is practical to use the technology. Nevertheless, facilities do not need to be outstanding in a computer-based environment. Case study evidence from the University of Cambridge shows that technical excellence does not necessarily guarantee that the technology will be used to maximal effect. Equally, if technology is seen as a useful part of the teaching and learning process, students and staff will overcome technical limitations to use it: this was found to be the case at Ulster.

An integrated infrastructure

This is needed to ensure a coherent framework for the use of technology in learning and teaching. It also ensures that the computer is not used in an isolated way. This was found to be a significant problem at Cambridge, where there was little sign of an infrastructure that integrated electronic communication with the other uses of computer technology, such as resource provision and class delivery and support. The Internet appears to offer such a coherent framework, either through the use of course or departmental websites (such as those in Toronto) or through a more controlled Virtual Learning Environment (VLE). VLEs, for example, are becoming more powerful and offer increasing opportunities for integrating external courseware and resources through them. The type of computer-based infrastructure used, though, will vary across institutions: local networks will work well in some cases, while the Internet or VLEs will prove effective in others.

Growing a culture

If staff and students are expected to use computer technology as part of their everyday learning and teaching experience, they need to see its relevance. Whereas more students than ever before come to university with a sound understanding of computer technology, that does not mean that they will be keen to use it as part of their learning experience. This highlights the importance of developing an electronic culture that makes the use of computer technology seem a natural part of university life for both staff and students. Ulster and Toronto have taken significant steps in developing an e-culture and theirs are good models to be followed. In other words, staff and students become so familiar with using computer technology in learning and teaching that they will use it instinctively.

Time

Creating a computer-based environment is a long-term objective. In the three case studies, the development of these environments has been ongoing since the mid 1990s and is still not near completion. It may take several years to ensure that the necessary hardware and software is in place. In addition, it will take time to change the learning and teaching culture to adapt to the use of technology. In some cases, this might mean that courses (or even the entire curriculum) needs to be re-structured and their contents changed. This will not take place overnight.

Human resources

A computer-based environment will not work without human resources. These resources take three forms: senior management, academic staff and support staff.

Senior management need to be prepared to support the creation of such an environment. Their support will encourage those grassroots staff who are already involved in the creation of electronic courseware and initiatives to keep up their work in this area. This type of support provides momentum for creating a computer-based environment.

One of the main forms of human resources is grassroots academic staff. Without them, the most proficient and advanced computer-based environment does not work. They need to be prepared to use technology in their teaching and encourage students to make use of it. Furthermore, academic staff need to feel that the use of a computer-based environment will prove beneficial and that the effort required to develop it will not prove an unnecessary burden. The University of Cambridge is a good example of how computer technology has not been totally embraced by grassroots staff because of the time and effort required to develop electronic courseware and e-learning resources.

Dedicated support staff are required to implement the environment. Ideally, these support staff will be more than technicians: they will be both computer specialists and also have some pedagogical knowledge and experience about the area of study that the environment is designed for. In a language-learning environment, for example, these support staff will have a good level of language proficiency. This means that these staff will be able to develop course-ware and resources themselves. As a result, the workload of already overburdened academic staff is not increased, and this, in turns, encourages many reluctant academics to use computer technology as part of their teaching. The impact of the excellent support infrastructure at Toronto on language teaching is a good example of this.

Strategic planning

A computer-based environment requires significant planning. A comprehensive plan will ensure that each of the above five recommendations are dealt with adequately. It will also involve bringing together all the technology-based teaching initiatives of individual staff under a coherent and integrated framework. If this structured and integrated approach does not exist, the development of computer-based environment will be patchy. The University of Toronto is a good illustration of this. There, the extent of the development of a computer-based language-learning environment varies across departments with some departments having made further progress in this area than others.

Facilitation of learning approaches

Each of the case studies demonstrated that computer technology can be used in both constructivist and behaviourist approaches to learning. In addition, each computer-based environment has used a combined approach on occasions, in an effort to maximise learning opportunities. An ideal learning environment, therefore, needs to offer all of these approaches to be effective.

Do they work?

The generally enthusiastic and positive reaction of staff and students from the institutions examined in this investigation indicates a widespread acceptance of the value of computer technology in language learning and teaching. Computer-based environments are, however, seen as deficient in the area of oral work.

In each institution studied, computer technology provides opportunities for a combination of constructivist and behaviourist approaches to learning that enable the acquisition of three main language skills: listening, reading and writing. Its use for oral work is less effective. As each of the case studies have shown, a computer-based environment allows students plenty of opportunities to read and listen to target language material, through the Web and CALL packages. In addition, students have also used e-mail and CALL programs to enhance writing opportunities. On the other hand, however, oral interaction does not yet take place through a computer, even though the technology is already in place to allow for oral interaction through CMC and video conferencing packages (some of which have been installed in the new multimedia labs at Ulster), although it is not widely used. In many cases, it is impractical to use computer technology for this because it requires real-time operation. It is more valuable for tandem experiments, although this requires the availability of adequate hardware and software in the partner institution(s). This is not always possible, especially when dealing with severely under-equipped universities, which are more common throughout mainland Europe than in either Britain or North America. As a result, until audiovisual CMC facilities are more commonly available in all universities, the potential for using computer technology for interactive oral work remains quite limited.

Aside from bringing pedagogical benefit, using a computer-based environment in language learning makes a difference in three other areas. Firstly, it improves communication between staff and students. This is particularly useful when they are dispersed across a wide area, making other forms of communication impractical. This is especially important for linguists, who need to communicate across different countries.

Secondly, an environment simplifies and improves the flexibility of information management, dissemination and processing. This makes it easier for students to adapt their study patterns around other commitments, such as part-time jobs. Furthermore, since language work is generally very intensive both in terms of time and work, this type of flexibility is even important in the context of language learning.

Finally, it is an ever-improving system. Computer-based environments will continue to evolve and develop through time. The environments studied in this investigation have not stopped developing and it has often been a difficult task to keep abreast with all these changes. As this investigation draws to an end, changes will have taken place to the environments in all three universities. However, in order to ensure a fair comparison between the three case studies, changes that have occurred in the 2002/03 academic year are not reported in this study. Improvements in computer technology over the past ten years have been astounding. These developments look set to continue, especially since in the area of artificial intelligence. These advances should provide better opportunities for using computer technology in oral work, which is currently a very deficient area in computer-based language-learning. Changes and improvements to computer-based environments allow learning and teaching methods to adapt to pedagogical and social change. At present, for example, a computer-based language-learning environment is flexible enough to cope with a sudden influx of new students and, equally, it is just as well equipped to deal with fewer students. These environments also bring (and in some cases, drag) language learning and teaching into an advanced technological era.

We can conclude, therefore, that computer-based environments make a difference to the language learning and teaching process, although they need to be carefully designed. It is crucial that the technology is integrated effectively into many aspects of the learning and teaching and that the technology becomes a natural and intuitive part of the learning and teaching experience. The primary role of these environments is to enhance and support learning and teaching and, as a result, the use of computer technology does not replace the role of either learner or teacher. Of course, some would argue that it is not essential to use such environments. Language learning and teaching can take place without computer technology, although the argument of this study is that there is general acceptance and support among staff and students for its use within teaching and learning and that its use is being seen increasingly as the norm, rather than the exception.

Future research

This study offers a number of options for potential future related research. An interesting comparison could be made of the three computer-based environments discussed in this work with the environments in the same institutions in five years time. A future study might show more advanced and highly developed environments. It would also report on the improvements made in computer technology and how these changes affect the language learning and teaching experience, especially teaching and learning oral skills. On a personal level, a comparative study in five years time would allow each institution to study the recommendations of this investigation and the examples of good and bad practice highlighted within it. The reaction and potential action taken by each university as a result, which would be reported in a future study, would be a useful test of the value of this work. Finally, a future study might also look at empirical evidence of the impact of computer technology on the language learning and teaching process. This study considers staff and student perception of its value. A future study would consider specific examples of how the computer makes a difference to learning by comparing the academic performance of students who use computer technology in their learning with a similar group who do not.

Bibliography

Adamson, R (1998). 'Modern language teaching and grammar: an explicit relationship?' In S Hotho (ed.), *Forum for Modern Languages Studies – Language Teaching and Learning: current trends in Higher Education*, 34 (2): Oxford University Press, 170–83

Allan, J (1990). 'Evaluating CALL'. In *Language Learning Journal* (2): 73–4

Arshad, F, Kelleher, G and Ward, P (1995). *Creating interactive learning environments: Delivering effective computer-based advice*, Sussex: Immediate Publishing

Atkinson, T (1991). 'IT in ITT: why use IT when chalk is hard to come by?' In *Language Learning Journal* (3): 63–7

Barr, D and Gillespie, J (2003). 'Creating a computer-based language-learning environment'. In *ReCALL* 15 (1): 68–78

Blackman, D (1984). 'Current status of behaviourism in learning theory'. In D Fontana (ed.), *Behaviourism and Learning Theory in Education*, 3–14

Bel, E and Ingraham, B (1997). 'Understanding the potential of the Internet for language teaching and learning'. In J Kohn, B Rüschoff & D Wolff (eds), *New Horizons in CALL, Proceedings of EUROCALL 1996*, EUROCALL, Szombathely, 103–18

Bennett, T J A (1989). 'Recent Developments in CALL'. In *Bulletin CILA* (49): 21–8

Besnard, C, Elkabas, C and Rosienski-Pellerin, S (1998). 'Students' empowerment: e-mail exchange and the development of writing skills'. In A Mollier (ed.), *Teaching and Learning Languages*, Toulon: Éditions Soleil, 385–94

Biesenbach-Lucas, S and Weasenforth, D (2001). 'E-mail and word processing in the ESL classroom: how the medium affects the message'. In *Language Learning & Technology*, 5 (1): 135–65

Blin, F (1995). 'Integrating CALL in the language curriculum: the SALL project'. In B Rüschoff & D Wolff (eds), *CALL & TELL in Theory and Practice: the Proceedings of EUROCALL 1994*, EUROCALL, Karlsruhe, 50–63

Boddy, D (1999). 'Barriers to electronic networking: technology, student needs or social context?' In *Active Learning* (10): 39–43

Boyd-Barnett, O and Scanlon, E (1991). *Computers and Learning*, Wokingham: Addison Wesley

Brammerts, H (1995). 'Tandem learning and the Internet: using new technology to acquire intercultural competence'. In A A Jensen *et al.* (eds). *Intercultural Competence: a New Challenge for Language Teachers and Trainers in Europe*, Denmark: Aalborg University Press, 209–22

Brierley, W and Kemble, W R (eds) (1991). *Computers as a Tool in Language Teaching*, Chichester: Ellis Horwood

Britain, S and Liber, O (2000). 'A framework for pedagogical evaluation of virtual learning environments'. In *JTAP* report. Accessed on the World Wide Web, February 2000: http://www.jtap.ac.uk/reports/htm/jtap-041.html

Bull, J and Zakrzewski, S (1997). 'Implementing learning technologies: a university-wide approach'. In *Active Learning* (6): 1-6

Burgess, G J A and Eastman, S (1997). 'Cybertrash or teaching tool? Or: untangling the Web: a critical look at using World Wide Web resources for Foreign Language Teaching and Learning'. In J Kohn, B Rüschoff & D Wolff (eds), *New Horizons in CALL, Proceedings of EUROCALL 1996*, EUROCALL, Szombathley, 157–68

Burnage, G (1999). 'Teachers and technicians: working together for effective use of information technology in language and literature'. In S Porter and S Sunderland (eds), *Teaching European Literature and Culture with Communication and Information Technologies*, Oxford: CTI Centre for Textual Studies, University of Oxford, 8–13

—— (2001). 'Approaches to university network-based language learning'. In *ReCALL*, 13 (2): 167–178

Bush, M and Terry, R (eds) (1997). *Technology-Enhanced Language Learning*, Illinois: National Textbook Co.

Byrnes, R, Dimbleby, J and Lo, B (1995). 'Flexible assignment submission in distance learning'. In J D Tinsley and T J van Weert (eds), *World Conference on Computers in Education VI: WWCCE '95 Liberating the Learner*, London: Chapman Hall, 305–15

Calvert, M (1992). 'Working in tandem: peddling an old idea'. In *Language Learning Journal* (6): 17–9

Cameron, K C (ed.) (1986). *Computers and Modern Language Studies*, Chichester: Ellis Horwood

Cash, D and St John, E (1995). 'German language learning via email: a case study'. In *ReCALL*, 7 (2): 47–51

Chase, R A (1974). 'Information Ecology and the Design of Learning Environments'. In G Coates (ed.), *Alternative Learning Environments*, Dowden, Pennsylvania: Hutchinson & Ross Inc., 282–96

Chen, M (1995). 'A methodology for characterising computer-based learning environments'. In *Instructional Science* (23): 183–220b

Coleman, J (1992). 'Project-based learning, transferable skills. Information technology and video'. In *Language Learning Journal* (5): 35–7

Conacher, J E and Royall, F (1998). 'An evaluation of the use of the Internet for the purposes of foreign language learning'. In *Language Learning Journal* (18): 37–41

Conway, K (1993). *Master classrooms: classroom design with technology in mind*, Chapel Hill: Institute for Academic Technology

Curtis, S A, Duchastel, J and Radic, N (1999). 'Proposal for an online language course'. In *ReCALL*, 11 (2): 38–45

Davies, G (2000). 'Lessons from the past, lessons for the future: 20 years of CALL'. Accessed on World Wide Web, August 2000: http://ourworld.compuserve.com/homepages/grahamdavies1/coegdd1.htm

Davies, T and Williamson, R (1998). 'The ghost in the machine: are "teacherless" CALL programs really possible?' In *Canadian Modern Languages Review*, 55 (1): 8–18

Davy, J (1984). 'Mindstorms in the lamplight'. In D Sloan, (ed.), *Computers in Education: a critical perspective*, London: Teachers College, 11–20

Desmarais, L (1998).'Le courrier électronique: un outil d'enseignant en milieu de travail'. In K Cameron (ed.), *Computer-Assisted Language Learning*, 12 (3): 323–44

Dunn, S and Morgan, V (1987). *The Impact of the Computer on Education: a Course for Teachers*, London: Prentice/Hall

Dyer, C A (1972). *Preparing for Computer-Assisted Instruction*, New Jersey: Educational Technology Publications

Elkabas, C, Trott, D and Wooldridge, R (1999). 'Contribution of the cybernautical approach to the teaching and learning of second languages (L2)'. In K Cameron (ed.), *Computer-Assisted Language Learning*, 12 (3): 241–54

Esch, E and Zähner, C (2000). 'The contribution of Information and Communication Technology (ICT): to language learning environments or the mystery of the secret agent'. In *ReCALL*, 12 (1): 5–18

Ehsani, F and Knodt, E (1998). 'Speech technology in computer-aided language-learning: strengths and limitations of a new CALL paradigm'. In *Language Learning & Technology*, 2 (1): 45–60

Felix, U (1999). 'Exploiting the Web for language teaching: selected approaches'. In *ReCALL*, 11 (1): 30–7

Fontana, D (ed.) (1984). *Behaviourism and Learning Theory in Education*, Edinburgh: Scottish Academic Press

Fox, M (1997). 'The teacher is dead! Long live the teacher! Implications of the virtual language classroom'. In *Active Learning* (7): 1–6

Frath, P (1995). 'What context for liberated computer-assisted language-learning?' In J D Tinsley & T J van Weert (eds), *World Conference on Computers in Education VI: WWCCE '95 Liberating the Learner*, London: Chapman Hall, 295–303

Garrett, N (1991). 'Technology in the service of language learning: trends and issues'. In *The Modern Language Journal*, 75, (1): 74–97

—— (1998). 'Computers in foreign language education: teaching, learning and language-acquisition research'. In *ADFL Bulletin*, 6–12

Gibbs, G (ed.), (1994). *Improving Student Learning: Theory and Practice*, Oxford: The Oxford Centre for Staff Development

Gillespie, J (1995). 'The integration of CALL tools into the Modern Languages Curriculum: a case study'. In B Rüschoff & D Wolff (eds), *CALL & TELL in*

229

Theory and Practice: the Proceedings of EUROCALL 1994, EUROCALL, Karlsruhe, 143–56

—— (2000). 'Towards a computer-based learning environment: a pilot study in the use of FirstClass'. In *ReCALL*, 12 (1): 19–26

Gillespie, J and Barr, D (2002). 'Reluctance, Resistance and Radicalism: A study of staff reaction towards the adoption of CALL/C&IT in modern languages departments'. In *ReCALL*, 14 (1): 120–32

Gillespie, J and McKee, J (1996). 'The Text Analysis Program: moving closer to the computer-based language classroom'. In A Gimeno (ed.), *Technology-Enhanced Language Learning in Theory and Practice: the Proceedings of EUROCALL 1995*, EUROCALL, Valencia, 133–46

—— (1998). 'The Text Analysis Program: Developing students' analytical skills'. In *ReCALL*, 10 (2): 44–52

—— (1999a). 'Resistance to CALL: degrees of student reluctance to use CALL and ICT'. In *ReCALL*, 11 (1): 38–46

—— (1999b). 'Does it Fit and Does it Make Any Difference? Integrating CALL into the Curriculum'. In *Computer-Assisted Language-Learning*, 12 (5): 441–55

Goodfellow, R, Jeffreys, I, Miles, T and Shirra, T (1996). 'Face-to-face language learning at a distance? A study of a videoconference try-out'. In *ReCALL*, 8 (2): 5–16

Goodfellow, R and Lamy, M-N (1998). 'Learning to learn a language – at home and on the Web'. In *ReCALL*, 10 (1): 68–78

Grega, W and Doughty D (1995). 'Open architecture environment for control engineering education'. In J D Tinsley & T J van Weert (eds), *World Conference on Computers in Education VI: WWCCE '95 Liberating the Learner*, London: Chapman Hall, 517–30

Green, S (1991). 'Experimenting with CALL'. In *Language Learning Journal* (3): 61–2

Grenfell, M (1997). 'Theory and practice in modern languages teaching'. In *Language Learning Journal* (16): 28–33

Hainline, D (1987). *New Developments in Computer-Assisted Language-Learning*, London: Croom Helm

Halliwell, S (1995). 'Grammar: identifying the key issues'. In *The Journal of the Northern Ireland Modern Languages Association* (28–33): 12–15

Hannafin, M J and Land, S M (1997). 'The foundations and assumptions of technology-enhanced student-centered learning environments'. In *Instructional Science* (25): 167–202

—— (2000). 'Student centred learning environments'. In D H Jonassen & S M Land (eds), *Theoretical foundations of learning environments*, London: Lawrence Erlbaum Associates, 1–23

Hare, G (1998). 'Using the World Wide Web as a resource in modern language studies'. In *Language Learning Journal* (18): 42–6

Harris, D (1999). 'Creating a complete learning environment'. In D French, C Hale, C Johnson & G Farr (eds). *Internet [Based] Learning: An introduction and framework for Higher Education and Business*, London: Kogan Page, 139–64

Hasan, H (1991). 'The paperless classroom'. In *Proceedings of ASCILITE – Simulation and Academic Gaming in Tertiary Education*, 267–76

Hawkins, E (1981). *Modern Languages in the Curriculum*, Cambridge: Cambridge University Press.

Haworth, W (1996). 'The Internet as a language learning resource'. In A Gimeno (ed.), *Technology-Enhanced Language Learning in Theory and Practice: the Proceedings of EUROCALL 1995*, EUROCALL, Valencia, 173–84

Heafford, M (1990). 'Teachers may teach, do learners learn?' In *Language Learning Journal*, March, 88–90

Higham, J (1992). 'Information Technology and modern languages in the National Curriculum'. In *Language Learning Journal* (5): 47–9

Hilgard, E R and Bower, G H (1966). *Theories of Learning*, 3rd ed. New York: Appleton-Century-Crofts

—— (1975). *Theories of Learning*, 4th ed. New Jersey: Prentice-Hall

Honebein, P, Duffy, T M and Fishman, B J (1993). 'Constructivism and the design of learning environments: context and authentic activities for learning'. In T M Duffy, J Lowyck, D H Jonassen & T M Welsh, (eds), *Designing environments for constructive learning*, London: Springer Verlag Berlin Heidelberg, 87–108

Howe, M J A (1984). *A Teacher's Guide to the Psychology of Learning*, Oxford: Basil Blackwell

Hudson, K (1984). *Introducing CAL: a Practical Guide to Writing Computer-Assisted Learning Programs*, London: Chapman and Hall

Iles, P (1994). 'Developing Learning Environments: Challenges for Theory, Research and Practice'. In *Journal of European Industrial Training*, 18, (3): 3–9

Jenkins, S-A and Servel-Way, M (1990). 'Doing IT meaningfully in Modern Languages'. In *Language Learning Journal*, September, 75–6

JISC (2000). Joint Information Systems Committee workshop final working report on Managed Learning Environments. Accessed through the World Wide Web, January 2001: http://www.jisc.ac.uk/pub00/mle/ final_rep.html

Johnson, L and S Lobello (eds), (1996). *The 21st Century Community College: Technology and the New Learning Paradigm*, New York: International Business Machines Co.

Jones, C (1986). 'It is not so much the program, more what you do with it: the importance of methodology in CALL'. In *System*, 14 (2): 171–78

Kailani, T Z (1995). 'A synthesized pedagogical methodology for English classroom interactions'. In *International Review of Applied Linguistics in Languages*, 33 (4): 333–44

Kassen, M and Higgins, C (1997). 'Meeting the technological challenge: introducing teachers to language-learning technology'. In M Bush and R Terry (eds), *Technology-Enhanced Language Learning*, 263–85

King, W E, Staczek, J J and Tolzman, A (eds), (1998). 'Integrating technology tools into the Language Curriculum'. In *Journal of Instruction Delivery Systems*, 12 (2): 14–8

Kohn, K (1995). 'Perspectives on computer-assisted language-learning'. In *ReCALL*, 7 (2): 5–19

Kötter, M, Shield, L and Stevens, A (1999). 'Real-time audio and e-mail for fluency: promoting distance language learners' aural and oral skills via Internet'. In *ReCALL*, 11 (2): 55–60

Laurillard, D (1993). *Rethinking University Teaching: a Framework for the Effective Use of Educational Technology*, London: Routledge

Leed, J (1995). 'A seven-step method for building effective learning environments'. In D Gayeski, (ed.), *Designing communication and learning environments*, New Jersey: Educational Technology Publications, 15–28

Levy, M (1996). 'Integrating CALL: The tutor and the tool'. In A Gimeno (ed.), *Technology-Enhanced Language Learning in Theory and Practice: the Proceedings of EUROCALL 1995*, EUROCALL, Valencia, 239–48

—— (1997). *Computer-Based Language Learning: Context and Conceptualization*, Oxford: Clarendon

—— (2000). 'Scope, goals and methods in CALL research: questions of coherence and autonomy'. In *ReCALL*, 12 (2): 170–95

Lewis, R and Tagg, D (eds), (1981). *Computers in Education*, Oxford: North Holland Publishing Co.

Lindgren, H C (1967). *Educational Psychology in the Classroom*, 3rd Ed, London: John Wiley & Sons Inc.

Longstaffe, M (1998). 'Language teaching on three different types of languages degrees'. In *The Journal of the Northern Ireland Modern Languages Association*, (16–19): 43–57

McCartan, A and Hare, C (1996). 'Effecting institutional change: the impact of some strategic issues in the use of IT'. In *ALT-J*, 4 (3): 21–8

McCarthy, B (1996). 'Fully integrated CALL: mission accomplished'. In *ReCALL*, 8 (2): 17–34

McDevitt, B (1997). 'Learner Autonomy and the need for learner training'. In *Language Learning Journal*, (16): 34–9

McLoughlin, C and Oliver, R (1998). 'Maximising the language and learning link in computer learning environments'. In *British Journal of Educational Technology*, 29 (2): 125–36

McKee, J (1995). 'The development of language acquisition skills through CALL: the Magee experiment'. In B Rüschoff & D Wolff (eds), *CALL & TELL in Theory and Practice: the Proceedings of EUROCALL 1994*, EUROCALL, Karlsruhe, 259–68

Marsh, D (1997). 'Project MERLIN: a learning environment for the future'. In *ReCALL*, 9 (1): 52–4

Martin, A (1997). 'Student IT induction: an evolving requirement'. In *Active Learning*, (6): 1–6

Meara, P (1994). 'The year abroad and its effects'. In *Language Learning Journal* (10): 32–8

Morley, D (1991). 'Teaching for learning – some reflections'. In *Language Learning Journal* (3): 50–2

Murray, D (2000). 'Changing technologies, changing literacy communities?' In *Language Learning & Technology*, 4 (2): 43–58

Murray, L (1994). Computer-Assisted Literary Research on Jean Paul Sartre's 'Les Mots' – a Presentation and Proposal Concerning the Development and Use of a Hypertext System, D.Phil Thesis, University of Ulster, Coleraine

NCIHE (1997). 'National Report–Communications and Information Technology'. In *The Dearing Report into Higher Education: Higher Education in the Learning Society*, National Committee of Inquiry into Higher Education: HMSO, (Chapter 13, Section 51). Accessed through the World Wide Web, June 2002: http://www.leeds.ac.uk/educol/ ncihe/nr_211.htm

Nicholson, B (1998). 'A case study of computer-based flexible learning using the World Wide Web and computer conferencing'. In *Language Learning Journal* – J, 6 (3): 38–46

Nisbet, J and Shucksmith, J (1986). *Learning Strategies*, London: Routledge

Northern Ireland Higher Education Council (1997). 'Reflections on Dearing' – Report of DENI/NIHEC Conference on Higher Education, October

Nott, D (1990). 'Modern Languages in Higher Education'. In *Language Learning Journal*, March, 44–7

Nwogu, K and Nwogu, E (1992). 'Computers and ESL in the West Midlands'. In *Language Learning Journal* (6): 74–6

O'Dowd, R (2000). 'Intercultural learning via videoconferencing: a pilot exchange project'. In *ReCALL*, 12 (1): 49–61

O'Neill, H F (ed.), (1978). *Learning Strategies*, London: Academic Press

—— (1981). *Computer-Based Instruction: a state of the art Assessment*, London: Academic Press

Oblinger, D G (1996). 'Creating a learning culture'. In L Johnson & S Lobello (eds), *The 21st Century Community College: Technology and the New Learning Paradigm*, New York: International Business Machines Co., 27–38

Orlandi, T (1999). 'European studies on formal methods in humanities'. In K de Smeld, H Gardiner, E Ore, T Orlandi, H Short, J Souillot and W Vaughan (eds), *Computing in Humanities Education*, Bergen: University of Bergen, 13–62

Oliva, M and Pollastrini, Y (1995). 'Internet resources and second language acquisition: an evaluation of virtual immersion'. In *Foreign Language Annals*, 28, (4): 551–63

Orsini-Jones, M (1999). 'Implementing institutional change for languages: online collaborative learning environments at Coventry University'. In *ReCALL*, 11(2): 61–73

Osuna, M and Meskill, C (1998). 'Using the World Wide Web to integrate Spanish language and culture: a pilot study'. In *Language Learning & Technology*, 1 (2): 71–92

Oxford Dictionary of Quotations: Expanded Edition (1995). Oxford: Oxford University Press

Paramskas, D (1993). 'Computer-assisted language-learning (CALL): increasingly integrated into an ever more electronic world'. In *The Canadian Modern Languages Review*, 50 (1): 124–43

Partee, M (1996). 'Using e-mail, web sites & newsgroups to enhance traditional classroom instruction'. In *T.H.E. Journal*, 23 (11): 79–82

Pellerin, M (1998). 'Ordinateurs: efficaces ou pas? (la perspective d'une enseignante)'. In K Cameron (ed.), *Computer-Assisted Language-Learning*, 12 (4): 381–90

Powell, B (1998). 'The use of computer-assisted language-learning'. In *Forum for Modern Language Studies*, 34 (2): 184–94

Pohjonen, J (1997). 'New learning environments as a strategic choice'. In *European Journal of Education*, 32 (4): 369–75

Raybould, T (1984). 'Precision Teaching and Pupils with Learning Difficulties'. In D Fontana (ed.), *Behaviourism and Learning Theory in Education*, 43–74

Reagan, T (1999). 'Constructivist epistemology and second/foreign language pedagogy'. In *Foreign Language Annals*, 32 (4): 413–25

Richardson, G (ed.), (1983). *Teaching Modern Languages*, London: Croom Helm

Richmond, I (1999). 'Is your CALL connected? Dedicated software vs integrated CALL'. In Cameron, K (ed.), *CALL: Media, Design and Applications*, Lisse: Swets & Zeitlinger, 295–314

Ross, M (1991). 'The CHILL factor (or computer-hindered language-learning).' In *Language Learning Journal* (4): 65–6

Salters, J and Reilly, C (1995). 'Communicative applications of computer-assisted language-learning'. In *The Journal of the Northern Ireland Modern Languages Association* (28–33): 21–5

Schweikhardt, W (1981). 'The impact of micro-computers on the education of blind students'. In R Lewis & E D Tagg (eds), *Computers in Education: Proceedings of the IFIP TC-3 3rd World Conference on Computers in Education*, New York: North Holland Publishing Co., 461–67

Sciarone, A G and Meijer, P J (1993). 'How free should students be? A case from CALL: computer-assisted language-learning'. In *Computers and Education*, 21, (1/2): 95–101

Scinicariello, S (1997). 'Uniting teachers, learners, and machines: Language Laboratories and other choices'. In M Bush and R Terry (eds), *Technology-Enhanced Language Learning*, 185–213

Selinger, M (1999). 'Opening up new teaching and learning spaces'. In T Evans and D Nation (eds), *Changing University Teaching: reflections on creating educational technologies*, London: Kogan Page, 85–97

Selinger, M and Pearson, J (1999). 'Linking different types of knowledge in professional education and training: the potential of electronic communication'. In M Selinger and J Pearson (eds), *Telematics in Education: trends and issues*, Oxford: Asevier Science, 15–31

Sloan, D (ed.), (1984). *Computers in Education: a critical perspective*, London: Teachers College

Sosabowski, M, Herson, K and Lloyd, A W (1998). 'Identifying and overcoming staff resistance to computer-based learning and teaching methods: shedding millstones to achieve milestones'. In *Active Learning* (9): 26–30

Stepp-Greany, J (2002). 'Student perceptions on language learning in a technological environment: implications for the new millennium'. In *Language Learning & Technology*, 6 (1): 165–80

Talbot, G (1996). 'Looking up in anger: translation practice in the CALL lab'. In *ReCALL*, 8 (1): 20–3

Taylor H G and Dupuis, R (1995). 'Community collaboration to develop active learning environments in school libraries through telecommunications'. In J D Tinsley & T J van Weert (eds), *World Conference on Computers in Education VI: WWCCE '95 Liberating the Learner*, London: Chapman Hall, 704–11

Wakely, R, Barker, A, Frier, D, Graves, P and Suleiman, Y (eds), (1995). *Language teaching and learning in Higher Education: issues and perspectives*, London: CILT

Wenger, G E (1996). 'Planning to take advantage of technology'. In L Johnson and S Lobello (eds), *The 21st Century Community College: Technology and the New Learning Paradigm*, New York: International Business Machines Co., 57–63

Wilson, J A R, Robeck, M C and Michael, W B (1969). *Psychological Foundations of Learning and Teaching*, 2nd ed., London: McGraw-Hill

Wintour, B and McDowell, B (1976). 'Automation at the New University of Ulster'. In Program, 10 (2): 60–74

Wolff, D (1997). 'Computer and New Technologies: Will they change language learning and teaching?' In J Kohn, B Rüschoff & D Wolff (eds), *New Horizons in CALL, Proceedings of EUROCALL 1996*, EUROCALL, Szombathley, 65–82

Woodin, J (1997). 'E-mail tandem learning and the communicative curriculum'. In *ReCALL*, 9 (1): 22–33

Woodin, J and Ojanguren, A (1997). 'E-mail tandem work for learning languages'. In J Kohn, B Rüschoff & D Wolff (eds), *New Horizons in CALL, Proceedings of EUROCALL 1996*, EUROCALL, Szombathley, 487–507

Woodruff, D (1961). *Basic Concepts of Teaching*, San Francisco: Chandler Publishing Co.

Wong, J and Fauverge, A (1999). 'LEVERAGE: Reciprocal peer tutoring over broadband networks'. In *ReCALL*, 11 (1): 133–42

Wyatt, D H (1984). *Computer-Assisted Language Instruction*, Oxford: Pergamon

Yazdani, M (1986). 'The ideal teaching machine'. In K C Cameron (ed.), *Computers and Modern Language Studies*, Chichester: Ellis Horwood, 144–51

Index